Michelle Popa
(86)

D1360522

Is something up there?

Dale White

SBS SCHOLASTIC BOOK SERVICES
New York Toronto London Auckland Sydney

Cover: Simulated photo by Cosimo Scianna

Copyright © 1968 by Doubleday and Company, Inc.
This edition is published by Scholastic Book Services,
a division of Scholastic Magazines, Inc., by arrangement
with Doubleday and Company, Inc.

3rd printing May 1970   Printed in the U.S.A.

Contents

Prologue

Good-bye, little green men?

Early in January 1969 the long-awaited report of a two-year study of flying saucers conducted by eminent scientists at the University of Colorado was made public. The investigation, financed by a federal grant, was undertaken at the request of the Air Force. The findings were minutely reviewed and approved by the National Academy of Sciences before being published under the title: *Scientific Study of Unidentified Flying Objects.*

Although it is difficult to describe briefly the conclusions reached in the bulky 1,456 page report, it states flatly that there is no evidence that UFOs are "spaceships from extraterrestrial civilizations." The Air Force, many scientists, and no doubt untold numbers of parents and teachers were relieved on reading this. Thank goodness, the pesky problem was settled once and for all!

For them the question *Is Something Up There?* was settled. Period.

However, saucer buffs howled with dismay. The staff at NICAP headquarters called a press conference and accused the scientists of ignoring the great mass of "reliable unexplained UFO sightings." So, the hot debate over whether UFOs are or are not visitors from outer space, which had simmered down while the study was in the making, promptly boiled over into new headings. The saucer supporters weren't one whit convinced. It didn't matter that one by one some of the most widely publicized sightings were shot down by scientific examination. People who witnessed some of the UFOs described in this book *know* what they saw. Besides, they point out gleefully, there are some sightings — particularly the McMinnville, Oregon, and Rex Heflin daytime photographs — which the scientists admit they could not explain and found puzzling. So there! The big question still looms overhead. Thus it would be folly to think we will hear no more about flying saucers.

The University of Colorado report made two stern recommendations. It advised closing out Project Blue Book, the Air Force investigation of UFO sightings, and rejected a civilian proposal that a federally supported "saucer agency" be established. The reason? "Our conclusion is that nothing has come from the study of UFOs in the past 21 years that has added to scientific knowledge."

Even young readers will feel the effects of this study, if teachers follow the suggestions made by Dr. Condon, director of the study, in an article

6

published in the February 1, 1969 issue of *The Saturday Review*. He strongly recommended "that teachers refrain from giving students credit for school work based on their reading of the presently available UFO books and magazine articles. Teachers who find their students strongly motivated in this direction should attempt to channel their interests in the direction of serious study of astronomy and meteorology, and in the direction of critical analysis of arguments for fantastic propositions that are being supported by appeals to fallacious reasoning or false data."

To this, the author heartily agrees. But, Dr. Condon, do we really have to say good-bye to the little green men and all those spine-tingling mysterious *Unexplainables*? We've had so much fun with them. Can't we ease them gently into the realm of science fiction? Maybe that's where they've belonged since that day in 1947 when Kenneth Arnold saw something up there.

1

Excitement at Exeter

VERY EARLY on the morning of September 3, 1965, teenager Norman Muscarello had the worst scare of his life. This is his story as he told it later.

Norman was hitchhiking along Route 150, a quiet country road in southeastern New Hampshire. Because he was to enter the Navy in three weeks, he had sold his car. Thus he was having to hike home after spending the evening with some friends in a neighboring community. There was little traffic after midnight so he caught few rides. By 2 A.M. he was still several miles from his home in the town of Exeter. The countryside was dark. There was no moon, but the night was exceptionally clear, the stars bright. There were no lights showing in the farmhouses he passed. Norman was not nervous because he had grown up in the area, and knew it well.

Suddenly, as he walked alongside a meadow

between two houses, he saw a huge object ringed
with brilliant red lights appear in the sky. It
looked bigger than the houses nearby. Norman
stopped. Then his heart began to pound as the
weird thing came closer and closer. It barely
skimmed some tall trees at the far end of the
meadow. It made no sound and wobbled quite a
bit. The lights blinked, bathing the field and
houses in a frightening red glow. The thing kept
coming on, looming larger and larger until Norman was positive it was going to hit him. With a
strangled cry, he dove down into the shallow
ditch beside the road. The object hovered over
his head for a few moments, and then slowly
backed off. It stopped over one of the houses,
the lights flared briefly, and it drew back still
farther. When it was about a hundred yards from
him, Norman scrambled to his feet and raced for
one of the houses.

"Help! Help! Let me in!" he shouted.

No one answered his frantic call.

Looking around in desperation, he saw car
lights approaching. He ran back to the road
and waved his arms. The car stopped. A man
called through the open window, "Something
wrong?"

Norman babbled his story. But when he turned
to point out the "thing" to the motorist, it had
disappeared. The red glow had faded. "I want to
get out of here! Take me to the police station."

The man looked at his wife, who was sitting
beside him. "This kid is really frightened. Maybe
we better do what he wants." He turned back to
Norman. "Hop in." Then he drove swiftly to the
police station at Exeter.

By the time they arrived, Norman had himself under better control. He walked in, identified himself, and said shakily, "You're not going to believe this, but I just saw a flying saucer!"

Officer Toland smiled. He figured this was some teenage prank. "Tell me about it," he said, offering Norman a chair. However, the longer the police officer listened to the seventeen-year-old's story, the more he became impressed with Norman's sincerity. Norman kept insisting that a policeman accompany him back to the scene. Feeling that the matter had better be investigated, Officer Toland called in a police cruiser.

Shortly after, Patrolman Eugene Bertrand appeared. He had an equally strange story to tell. He said, "The darndest thing just happened. I was cruising two miles out of town when I saw a car parked by the road, and a woman sitting in it. She was alone. I stopped and asked her if everything was all right. You know what she said? She claimed that a huge silent flying object had trailed her car for over ten miles as she drove from Epping toward Exeter. She said at times it was only a few feet away, and she could see its red pulsating lights, then it zoomed away."

Officer Toland asked Bertrand, "Why didn't you radio in about it?"

The patrolman grinned. "I thought the woman was a kook! Anyway, she said she was over her scare, and drove away."

Toland turned to Norman. "Does that woman's story sound familiar?"

Norman nodded vigorously. "Yes, sir. She described the very same thing I saw."

After Norman repeated his story to the patrolman, Officer Toland said, "You two drive out to where Norman says he saw this thing. Check out the area, and then report in." He knew that the patrolman had served in the Air Force in Korea before becoming a police officer, and was a thoroughly reliable, level-headed person, with a better than average knowledge of aircraft.

The two left in the police car. When they reached the meadow, Norman said, "Stop here."

Bertrand did. "I don't see anything."

"It was over there," Norman said, pointing to the open field between the two houses.

"Let's take a look." Bertrand called the station, reported he was going for a short walk, and would be absent from the car.

Flashlight in hand, the policeman and the teenager walked across the meadow. Nearby was a corral where the horses on the Carl Dining farm were kept. As the men approached, all was quiet. But suddenly the horses began to kick and whinny loudly. And then slowly, silently, a huge lighted object rose up from behind two tall trees. It drifted toward them, wobbling as Norman had seen it do earlier. As its lights brightened, a red glow enveloped the white farmhouses on each side of the meadow.

Norman was paralyzed with fright. After the first shock, Bertrand pulled him back to the police car. Both got in, and Bertrand contacted the police station. "I see it!" he shouted into the hand microphone. "I see it myself!"

The UFO, as he called it (the standard abbreviation for Unidentified Flying Object), was about the length of a football field away from him, and about a hundred feet above ground, though it was difficult to judge accurate distances at night. It seemed to be rocking back and forth. The red lights around the rim pulsated from left to right, then right to left, 1-2-3-4-5, 5-4-3-2-1. These lights were so dazzlingly bright that Bertrand could not make out any definite shape of the craft. "It's like looking into car headlights turned high, and guessing what model it is."

"Keep an eye on it, and call back," Officer Toland ordered.

Meantime Patrolman David Hunt in another police cruiser had heard Bertrand's exciting report on his car radio. He dashed to the scene and joined his associate. Bertrand was relieved to see him. "Check us out so Toland won't think we're imagining things."

After one long look, Hunt gasped, "I can't believe it!"

The UFO suddenly began to flutter from right to left. Then it darted and dashed in short spurts, turned sharply, speeded up, slowed down, and hovered. The three men were stunned by the performance because they had never seen an aircraft fly as strangely as this one.

Bertrand said positively, "That's no conventional aircraft."

"If it isn't a plane, what is it?" Norman asked, his voice shrill. "It's real. We're not imagining it. What bugs me is it doesn't make any noise." He shivered, although the night was warm.

All three of them were very familiar with aircraft since Pease Air Force Base was only twelve miles away at Portsmouth. Almost everyone in the surrounding area, even Exeter schoolchildren, could identify B-47s, B-52s, jet fighters, commercial airliners, and helicopters.

Norman and the two policemen talked constantly while watching the UFO's weird antics, wondering whether it was some sort of secret revolutionary weapon the government was developing. It could have been, except no American aircraft, known or secret, would dare violate the air traffic safety laws laid down by the Federal Aviation Agency. The UFO was flying far too low for safety. They all agreed that the chance of its being an enemy secret weapon was practically zero, since our military radar surveillance was never relaxed.

"Secret or not, the design is sure revolutionary," Hunt said. "It has no visible motors or propellers, and no wings."

"But it does have a tail fin, or something like that," Norman pointed out. "Look hard. You can catch a glimpse of the fin when it tilts."

"Maybe it's one of those flying saucers from outer space," one of them suggested half seriously.

The other two snorted. Flying saucers were for crackpots and science fiction fans. But after watching the UFO perform some more, all agreed reluctantly, "It sure acts like someone, or something, is piloting it."

Then, as unexpectedly as it had appeared, the UFO slipped out of sight, flying due east toward the Atlantic Ocean. A few moments later, a plane droned overhead.

"That's a B-47," Bertrand said at once. They listened to its roaring engines as it passed over in a smooth, direct-line flight. They remarked how differently this conventional aircraft behaved, as compared to the UFO.

When they returned to the cars, Norman said,

"Hey, I better get home. My mother will be worried stiff about me."

Bertrand and Hunt reported in to headquarters that they were taking Norman home. The boy was right. His mother was awake and worried. When she saw two police officers escorting her son up the stairs to the family apartment, she knew something terrible must have happened.

Norman told her about his big scare. She could not believe it. The two officers assured her that her son was telling the truth.

The two patrolmen soon left. Hunt resumed his patrol duties. Bertrand drove to headquarters and gave Officer Toland the full story. Then Bertrand sat down at a desk and typed out a report, which he signed. When he finished, it was time for him to go off duty.

Lieutenant Warren Cottrell took over the police desk from Officer Toland at 8 A.M. The first thing he did was to read Bertrand's report. Next he reported the sighting of an unidentified flying object to Pease Air Force Base at Portsmouth. That afternoon two officers from the base arrived and questioned everybody involved. They also checked out the location where the sighting had been made and the reputations of Norman and the two police officers. Satisfied that the sightings were not a prank or a hoax, they returned to the base without making any comment.

All this time things were anything but dull at the police station. The telephone rang constantly as dozens of people reported they had seen the bright wobbling UFO. Reporters from the Exeter newspaper and radio station gathered information for feature stories. Calls were received from

newspaper editors in outlying communities who
had received reports of sightings in their areas
and wanted to check their information against
the Exeter report. Television stations throughout
New England broadcasted the news. As always
happens after news of a UFO sighting is released
to the public, many more people called in to say
that they, too, had seen a UFO.

Usually when a UFO is observed, it is seen
only once or twice within a very short period of
time. The astonishing part about the Exeter incident was that there was much more to come.

Apparently just about everybody in Exeter
talked flying saucers that day, and for many days
afterward. His friends kidded Norman so much
that he vowed to spend every night until he left
for the Navy watching for the UFO. He was determined to see it again. Several of his pals offered to keep him company. Some nights his
mother was along. Other nights she went watching with some friends. All did see a UFO at
varying times later, though at a greater height
and distance. Every night for weeks the roads
around Exeter were lined with cars filled with
"saucer watchers." Some people vowed they saw
one or more. Others saw "strange lights." Several were positive they saw Air Force jets chas-
ing a "glowing orangeish ball" that constantly
outpaced them. At least two people reported a
daytime sighting.

The stack of reports filed with the police grew
higher and higher. Restaurants and motels did
an increased business as people from neighboring communities and other New England states
flocked to Exeter in the hope of seeing a real

flying saucer. All were intensely curious and excited, and none were frightened. Their attitude seemed well expressed by one teenage girl who gushed, "Isn't it absolutely the spookiest thing ever, and so exciting!"

The talk boiled anew when another teenager named Ron Smith saw a UFO. Both adults and teenagers considered Ron a "good kid" — the kind who made average grades in high school, was fun and friendly, kept out of trouble, and worked in the grocery store after school and on Saturdays. Night after night he had driven his mother and aunt around, looking for the "thing." One evening when they were fairly near the same Dining farm where Norman had seen the UFO before, Ron's aunt exclaimed, "Stop the car! I see something."

After one look, Ron braked hard. He turned out the headlights so he could see better and leaned out the window. He gazed up at something that had a red light on top, a glowing white bottom, and was spinning. As Ron watched open-mouthed, it slipped past the car. He twisted to watch it. It stopped in midair, reversed, and went back over the car, stopped again, passed over the car again, and then took off in a streak of light.

"Wow! We better report this to the police!" Ron exclaimed. His mother and aunt were as excited as he was. Ron drove toward town. But when they were halfway there, he stopped.

"What's the matter?" Mrs. Smith asked.

"I'm going back to make sure that thing was there. I've got to be sure I wasn't seeing things."

"You weren't imagining it. We saw it too."

Nevertheless, Ron went back, and there it was.

It looked the same and passed over the car once before disappearing. This time Ron and his aunt got a better look. Both agreed the UFO was oval, white in the center and red around the rim, and bigger than a B-52. Ron thought he heard a humming noise, "sort of like a cat purring." The UFO tilted at times, but he could not see any wings. It most definitely was not a meteor, nor a helicopter, nor a regular plane. It was the stop-start-reverse movements that shook Ron. He had the creepy feeling that someone just had to be piloting it!

When the UFO did not return, Ron drove to the police station. He and his mother and aunt made their reports. The officer on duty typed out the details, and added them to the other reports.

A weird and different sighting was made by sixteen-year-old Joseph Jalbert. Joseph had done a lot of sky-watching after what had happened to Norman and Ron. The Jalbert home was very close to power lines that ran along Route 107. One evening he was outside looking around, not really expecting to see anything, but hoping he would. Suddenly he saw a reddish, cigar-shaped object very high in the sky. His mouth fell open even farther when he watched a smaller reddish object emerge from the bigger one, and slowly descend toward earth. When the smaller object was not more than two hundred feet from him, it hovered over the power lines. Then a sort of pipe came out of it, contacted one power line for a few seconds, and slowly drew back inside. After that the smaller object, which Joseph thought looked like a disc, sped skyward and disappeared inside the cigar-shaped craft!

After he recovered from his surprise, Joseph rushed into the house and spilled the story to his parents. They ran outside but could see nothing. Later the boy told his story to the police.

By this time the Exeter sightings had received nationwide publicity. John Fuller, a noted author, described the incident in his regular column in the *Saturday Review* magazine. Then he had a great idea. As far as he knew, and he had followed UFO sighting reports for years, no one had ever made a thorough examination of a good sighting made by numerous people at fairly close range. He felt the Exeter story would be perfect to investigate because it involved so many people in one small area. Mr. Fuller visited Exeter and interviewed over sixty people who claimed to have sighted a UFO. He used a tape recorder so he could go over each story and check it for contradictions. Everyone cooperated fully.

After this Mr. Fuller wrote a long article about the Exeter sightings. It was first published in *Look* magazine on February 8, 1966, under the title "Outer-Space Ghost Story." It was reprinted in the May 1966 issue of *The Reader's Digest*. It created a sensation. After that Mr. Fuller expanded his material into an exciting book entitled *Incident at Exeter*. It was well received by many readers. However, others, including Walter Sullivan, Science Editor of *The New York Times*, considered some of the book's contents "preposterous."

The account of the Exeter sightings in this chapter is based on information in Mr. Fuller's book, which emphasizes the human interest rather than the scientific side of the UFO furor at

Exeter. Mr. Fuller did not try to prove that what had been seen at Exeter were vehicles from outer space. He felt that this theory was one of several possible explanations to be explored further.

The Air Force, which has been investigating American UFO sightings for twenty years, issued an official explanation of the Exeter sightings in a statement published in a Washington, D.C., newspaper on October 27, 1965. This statement said that the several reports stemmed from "multiple objects in the area," which meant that a high-altitude Strategic Air Command exercise was going on at that time over the area and people had mistaken the planes for UFOs. The statement also gave as another possible explanation the existence of a common weather condition known as a "weather inversion," wherein a layer of cold air is trapped between layers of warm air. The Pentagon spokesman explained that this natural phenomenon causes stars and planets to appear to dance and twinkle and concluded, "We believe what the people saw that night were stars and planets in unusual formation."

The people of Exeter rejected this explanation, as did Mr. Fuller. He talked with officers from Pease Air Force Base who said privately and off-the-record that they did not agree with it. A careful check with Strategic Air Command people showed that the high-altitude exercise was over and the planes withdrawn by 2 A.M., whereas the two patrolmen and Norman Muscarello had made their joint sighting at about 3 A.M. A check with Weather Bureau personnel revealed that there was no temperature inversion in the area at that time.

Patrolmen Bertrand and Hunt felt that the Pentagon explanation practically called them liars. They wrote the Air Force a letter, which Mr. Fuller published in his book and which said in part, "What bothers us most is that many people are thinking that we were either lying or not intelligent enough to tell the difference between what we saw and something ordinary."

On February 9, 1966, John P. Spaulding, Lieutenant Colonel U. S. Air Force, Chief of the Civil Branch Community Relations Division Office of Information, wrote the two: "Based on additional information which you submitted to our UFO investigation office at Wright-Patterson Air Force Base, Ohio, we have been unable to identify the object you observed on September 3, 1965."

The Exeter story is only one of many reports of American sightings, yet there has been an enormous amount of publicity over this one case. There are several reasons for this. One, it captured the imagination of thousands of Americans, young and old, because it was spectacular and very exciting. Two, it was a strong low-altitude multiple sighting made by numerous people who all can't have been mistaken about what they saw. Three, thanks to John Fuller, the sightings were given serious consideration and were not brushed off as nonsensical hallucinations. Four, the Exeter affair revealed the confusion and lack of coordination and disagreements that characterize the investigation of UFO sightings in the United States today. And five, the public concern may have helped bring about a much-needed new chapter in the study of unidentified flying objects.

2

A Short History
of Flying Saucers

UFO SIGHTINGS have made headlines in the
United States for twenty years. Two principal
agencies are specially charged with investigating
them in this country. One is the United States Air
Force. The other is the National Investigations
Commission on Aerial Phenomena (NICAP), an
independent private organization not connected
in any way with the U. S. Government.

Occasionally a writer such as Mr. Fuller, or a
newspaper reporter, or an astronomer, or a physicist studies one or more sightings independently.
But for steady long-range investigation, the Air
Force and NICAP have made the most significant
contributions. Neither agency has solved the mystery of UFOs so far, but both are bringing more
scientifically trained people into the effort.

The Air Force relies on investigations made by
its own people and numerous other government
agencies involved in aerial studies, such as weather and radar bureaus. Sometimes it calls on civilian scientific experts, such as astronomers and

physicists, to evaluate the evidence it has gathered. It does not open its files to the public, but does cooperate with qualified reporters. It issues a statement only when it can say positively that such-and-such a UFO was really a twinkling star, a meteor, a satellite, burning marsh gas, a conventional aircraft, or one of countless other explainable phenomena. The nation's radar defense informs the Air Force of the approach of any unidentified flying object, and our secret agents abroad keep the Air Force posted on experimental foreign aircraft so these will not be mistaken for UFOs. The Air Force takes the position that all UFOs really are natural objects or phenomena which can be explained when enough information about them is furnished. It strongly rejects the possibility that even one of the thousands of UFOs sighted could be an interplanetary ship.

The second agency, NICAP, was founded in 1956 and has no connection with the government. Its membership is made up largely of civilians who volunteer their services for checking on sightings. NICAP's activities will be described in the next chapter. Richard Hall, Assistant Director of NICAP, stated this agency's position well when he told John Fuller, "We have carefully considered all the evidence we have, and we support the hypothesis that UFOs are under intelligent control — and that some of them might be of extraterrestrial origin." In other words NICAP takes the position that some UFOs *could* be spaceships from another planet.

From the very beginning UFO investigations have been riddled with arguments, contradictions, unwise public statements, and sensationalism. The

arguments never cease because UFO's are like
fleas on a dog — they are universal, they appear
without rhyme or reason, they annoy and dis-
tract and are impossible to catch. They pop up
unexpectedly all over the world, and keep investigators and amateur guessers in a constant state
of exasperation and puzzlement.

Why are many people fascinated by UFOs?
Well, partly because they remain a big mystery,
sometimes a shivery, spooky, spine-tingling, eye-
popping kind of mystery. Partly because five mil-
lion persons have seen what they believed were
UFOs (according to a recent Gallup poll.) Maybe
another reason is that sighting a UFO could happen to anyone. Aborigines in Australia have
seen them, as well as people in Russia and the
Far East, farm hands in South America, pilots
flying the Arctic and Antarctic, and thousands
of ordinary citizens in Europe and North America. These sightings add up to a whopping space-
age mystery story, and almost everyone, young
and old, likes a mystery. Flying saucers pose
some knotty problems, but they are also great
fun.

Actually, man's awareness of unidentified flying objects goes back many centuries. The Old
Testament tells us that the prophet Ezekiel saw a
fiery flying wheel in the sky. In 100 B.C. a Latin
poet named Julius Obsequiens wrote, "At sunset
a circular object like a shield was seen to sweep
across the sky from West to East." Numerous
other sightings have been chronicled down
through the centuries.

One of the earliest American sightings on record took place on November 23, 1896. Thousands

of people watched a strange cigar-shaped object move slowly eastward across the sky from Oakland, California, to Chicago. For lack of another word in that preaviation era, reporters called it an "airship." A few more such objects were reported in the 1920s and 1930s. During World War II and the Korean War, combat pilots and their crews out on bombing raids frequently observed mysterious lights zipping about, which became so common that the pilots jokingly called them "foo fighters." No one ever discovered what they were.

Then on Tuesday, June 24, 1947, Kenneth Arnold, a businessman from Boise, Idaho, was flying his private plane in the vicinity of Mount Rainier, Washington. About 3 P.M. he saw nine shiny silver discs playing tag about the great snowy peak. They were smaller than an airliner, but lacked visible engines or tail fins. They spun and turned in a way that would have wrecked any conventional aircraft. By noting time lapse and distance, Mr. Arnold figured their speed at about 1,700 miles per hour. Before he could close in on them, the flying discs sped out of sight.

After landing, Mr. Arnold reported his sighting to airport employees and a newspaper reporter. When asked to describe the discs' appearance, he is supposed to have said they looked like saucers that were flying. The newspaper played up the phrase "flying saucers." Other newspapers all across the country and even abroad picked up the story. The phrase caught on. Adults grinned, and children laughed delightedly at the idea of flying saucers zipping about overhead. Mr. Arnold became famous overnight, but not in a way he liked.

Practically everyone accused him of pulling a hoax. No one took him seriously. The more he protested that he had seen flying saucers, the more people laughed. He was beset with crank telephone calls, and branded a liar. For a veteran pilot and man of good reputation who had never been involved in a hoax, this hurt.

Mr. Arnold lashed out at his taunters. "Call me Einstein, or Flash Gordon, or just a screwball — I'm absolutely certain of what I saw! But believe me, if I ever see again a phenomenon of that sort in the sky, even if it's a ten-story building flying through the air, I won't say a word about it!"

Mr. Arnold's story seems even more remarkable if you remember that it broke in 1947, at a time when guided missiles, supersonic speed, satellites, astronauts, moon landings, and space walks existed only in tales of science fiction, or in the exploits of cartoon characters like Buck Rogers and Flash Gordon.

Of course, the Arnold story was brought to the attention of Air Force officials. It was imperative that they know if the flying unknowns posed a threat to our national security. The Aerospace Technical Intelligence Center (ATIC) at Wright-Patterson Air Force Base, was alerted to follow up the story. Since ATIC was responsible for keeping track of all foreign aircraft activities, it sent experts to question Mr. Arnold.

After studying the information he gave them, the ATIC team could not say positively what it was Mr. Arnold had seen. One officer guessed the discs were a mirage or an optical illusion. Another thought they were birds or possibly "grindstone" clouds. These are clouds shaped like enormous discs and often seen piled together.

Reporters asked, "Could the discs be secret weapons our government is testing?"

The ATIC officers answered, "We have no experimental craft of that nature. We are completely mystified."

"Could they be Russian secret weapons?"

The investigators had no answer to that, and returned to their headquarters.

Mr. Arnold rejected all their explanations. He insisted then, and still says, "I did see flying discs."

The Arnold story seemed to set off a chain of other reports. Air bases all over America were flooded with calls from people who claimed they saw flying lights, flying saucers, flying tear drops, and even flying pie plates! Then Air Force people themselves began to see flying objects.

On June 28, 1947, at 3:15 P.M. an Air Force pilot flying near Lake Mead, Nevada, saw five unidentified flying objects. That same night at 9:30 P.M. a bright light was observed in the air near Maxwell Air Force Base at Montgomery, Alabama. This time two intelligence officers, two pilots, and four Air Force officers saw it. The light zigzagged, streaked about at high speed, and made a sharp ninety-degree turn before disappearing. The observers agreed it could not have been a star or a meteor.

On July 8, 1948, a round object was sighted by a test pilot at 10:10 A.M. over the super-secret Air Force Test Center in California's Mojave Desert. It seems certain the pilot was not trying to put over a hoax, for he had an excellent record. He had no mental quirks, nor was he overtired. He was well briefed in high-altitude winds and weather balloon performances. Still, he reported seeing a round object, yellow-white in color, moving about two hundred miles an hour *against* the wind. Others saw it too, and confirmed his descriptions.

At 11:50 A.M. on that same day and in that same place five Air Force technicians observing an aerial seat-ejection experiment spotted an object. These men had been screened carefully before being assigned their task. They were considered sound and reliable. Their written report of the sighting stated, "It presented a distinct oval-shaped outline, with two projections on the upper surface which might have been thick fins or nobs. These crossed each other at intervals, suggesting either rotation or oscillation of slow type. No smoke, flames, propeller arcs, engine noise, or other plausible or visible means of propulsion were noted." The object was silver-colored, like aluminum. The report concluded, "It was man-made, as evidenced by the outline and functional appearance. Seeing this was not a hallucination."

The Air Force is charged with the responsibility of securing the nation's aerial defense against enemy aircraft or aerial invasion. Thus it found itself catapulted into an investigative program. Too many unidentified flying objects were being sighted over military bases and defense installations. The difficult task was turned over to the Aerospace Technical Intelligence Center. Housed in a Quonset hut behind a barbed-wire enclosure at Wright-Patterson Air Force Base, ATIC's actual staff was small. Fortunately it was impowered to request assistance from intelligence officers at every air base, and the Air Defense Command as well. The staff did very well, considering it was handed a big, strange project for which it had no background information and no previous experience on which to base its investigations. Because some of the information undoubtedly would be of interest to an enemy nation, tight security measures were clamped down. The findings were kept secret for many years.

Even at these early dates of 1947 and 1948, Air Force authorities were deeply concerned over public reaction to flying saucers. At first the reports were greeted with hoots and laughter. But as hundreds more poured in from all over the nation, newspapers and irresponsible citizens began to hint darkly that maybe our country was being "invaded" by creatures from outer space, or being threatened by Russian secret weapons. Many people became alarmed. The Air Force was determined to prevent panic from developing. Its officials remembered only too well what had happened about ten years earlier when an ugly panic gripped the nation momentarily.

At that time, 1938, there was no television, so millions of Americans listened nightly to favorite radio programs. One evening a nationwide radio network presented a very dramatic, suspenseful play about a fancied invasion of the earth by men from Mars. The play starred Orson Welles and was very realistic. Unfortunately thousands of people tuned in a little tardily, or didn't pay close attention to the opening announcement, and

did not realize they were listening to a play. They
thought they were listening to an on-the-spot report of an actual invasion occurring that very
minute. Many panicked. They grabbed guns, ran
screaming into the streets, fired indiscriminately,
snarled traffic, and created an uproar. Police stations, airports, and military bases were so flooded
with telephone calls that communications bogged
down. As soon as the network realized what panic
its radio play had triggered, it went all-out to
reassure listeners there was no invasion and no
cause for alarm. But it was hours before calm
was restored.

Thus, recalling this unfortunate happening, the
Air Force made every effort through its public
statements to reassure the nation that it was making a determined effort to solve the mystery of
the unidentified flying objects and was maintain-
ing a strong aerial alert and defense, so there
was no need for panic. This effort paid off. People
were relieved and content to leave the matter in
the capable hands of the Air Force.

Americans generally had faith in their government and its military services. They did not panic
in 1947. They have never become unduly worried
about flying saucers, even though numerous
books and articles have taken the position that
some unidentified flying objects are interplanetary spaceships.

To give you a small idea of how complex an
investigation can be and how many skilled people
can be involved, here are summaries of just a few
of the inquiries made by the ATIC staff in 1947.

A major concern was whether or not these
strange objects were secret weapons. Since U.S.

engineers did not possess the know-how to produce such revolutionary aircraft, authorities worked on the assumption that such craft might have been built by another country, possibly the U.S.S.R. Word went out to agents stationed in Germany and Russia to find out if Russia did possess advanced-design spacecraft. Although many weeks passed before the answers trickled back, the report was a reassuring no.

Could these objects be one of our own secret weapons? Again, after much quiet investigation, the answer was no.

The staff checked out weather reports for the areas where the sightings had been noted, to learn if clouds, temperature inversions, or mirages might have caused optical illusions. They checked with astronomers at observatories as to the location of the brighter stars and planets. They charted the courses of weather balloons aloft at that time. They even considered the possibility that the discs might have been high-flying geese, gulls, or eagles whose feathers reflected sunlight. They gathered reports on the location of all civilian, commercial, and military planes in the air close to the sighting areas.

They asked a number of topflight scientists, "What do you think these unidentified flying objects are?" The scientists said they did not have enough of the right kind of information on which to base opinions.

The ATIC staff ran character checks on those who had observed the strange objects. A high percentage of the sightings had come from military and commercial pilots. These men had logged hundreds of hours of flying time and were

familiar with clouds, stars, and other aerial phenomena. All had been trained to be alert, exact,
and unexcitable in emergencies. Pilots had to be
in top physical condition and were not permitted
to drink alcohol from twenty-four to forty-eight
hours before flying. No pilot would want to injure
his reputation by pulling a hoax or a cheap publicity stunt. However, while accepting much pilot
information as reliable, the ATIC men also kept
in mind that even well-trained, reliable witnesses
can sometimes make mistakes.

The staff also asked the Air Force Aeromedical
Laboratory if a human body could withstand the
speeds and sharp turns noted in some flying
saucer gyrations. The answer was no. As a further check on the possible existence of the saucers,
the ATIC staff contacted plane manufacturers
and asked, "Could a disc-shaped craft be built
by the principles of aerodynamic engineering we
now know? If so, could its material stand up under
such fantastic speeds and turns?" The answer to
both questions was again no, and so far no engineering discovery has turned up to contradict that
finding.

Although the number of sightings dropped
temporarily after August 1948, the ATIC people
worked on. Their experts and their superior officers were confident that, within a year at the
most, they would have the answer to the puzzling
riddle.

How wrong they were! The sightings at Exeter,
New Hampshire, and those before and after,
have made it very clear that Americans are no
nearer the solution in 1968 than they were twenty
years ago.

3

The Air Force Position

On January 22, 1948, the Air Force investigation of flying saucers was centralized in one project under the code name of "Sign." Its findings were restricted to security military use; that is, the information was available only to certain Air Force officials. In time, as the Air Force refined its investigative methods, the project was renamed "Grudge," for reasons not given. In the spring of 1952 the name was changed to "Project Blue Book." The Aerospace Technical Intelligence Center remained in charge but was referred to more commonly as the Air Technical Intelligence Center.

Since numerous sightings did not fit the description of "flying saucers," the Air Force officially changed to a more inclusive term, that of unidentified flying objects. The term was often shortened to UFOs, pronounced yoo-foes.

As we said in Chapter 1, the Air Force has scored some fine successes in identifying UFOs. It

has had some failures, too. Some sightings had to
be labled "Unknown" or "Unexplained." The
stories about these solved and unsolved sightings
make exciting reading. However, since the Air
Force may say one thing at first and something
different later on, and the NICAP information
may point to yet another conclusion, the ordinary
citizen can easily become confused and wonder
who was right. The Air Force has changed its
position on UFOs from time to time. Sometimes
it has issued contradictory statements, as in the
Exeter case. Actually, it was dissatisfaction with
these Air Force statements that helped bring
about the formation of NICAP.

Reading only one exciting story after another
without knowing the background of the investigative agencies is like trying to hang up clothes
with clothespins but no clothesline! Let's get that
"line" — the background — stretched first, and afterward hang the separate stories on it.

In 1947 and 1948 the position of the Air
Force was one of openminded and concerned inquiry. The general public waited patiently for an
official statement which would put an end to the
mystery. No one realized then that such a statement was impossible. The Air Technical Intelligence Center staff urged those reporting UFOs to
get all the factual evidence possible. This included
information about their size, shape, behavior, and
other physical characteristics, radar sightings,
and, if possible, photographs. Military pilots who
observed UFOs were told to alert the nearest air
base immediately by radio so that additional
competent observers, either on the ground or in

the air, might assist in identifying the UFO. Thus many sightings by qualified and reliable witnesses were reported. But these still did not point to a positive identification for all UFOs. Why not?

The reason is explained officially by Lieutenant Colonel Lawrence J. Tacker in *Flying Saucers and the U. S. Air Force,* a book he wrote while serving as an Air Force Public Information Officer. Lieutenant Colonel Tacker wrote, "However, each incident seemed to have unsatisfactory facts associated with it, such as shortness of time under observation, inaccurate estimates of distances from the observer, the vagueness of descriptions, or lack of photographs, inconsistency between individual observers, and a serious lack of descriptive data that prevented definite conclusions from being drawn. Explanations of some of the incidents revealed the existence of simple and easily understandable causes so that there appeared initially the possibility that enough incidents could be solved to eliminate or greatly reduce the aura of mystery already associated with the sightings."

In other words, two things became increasingly obvious: There was enough information to prove that many UFOs were real objects and known aerial phenomena, but there was not enough of the right kind of information to solve all sightings.

In September 1948 Air Force officials asked ATIC experts to prepare an "Estimate of the Situation." They wanted to know what conclusion ATIC experts had reached so far regarding the nature of UFOs. The estimate was put together, labeled "Top Secret," and sent on to the Air

Force Chief of Staff, General Hoyt S. Vandenberg. The ATIC conclusion was that *some UFOs were interplanetary spaceships*.

After a number of Pentagon officials read it, the estimate was fired back. Why? Because the top officers felt that the estimate was based largely on personal opinion and not supported by concrete facts.

If this was all "Top Secret," how do we know about it today? The reason is that much of the information gathered by ATIC during these early years was later declassified; that is, it was decided that it need not be kept secret any longer. From September 1951 to September 1953, Captain Edward J. Ruppelt was Chief of Project Blue Book. After he retired from the post, Captain Ruppelt wrote a lively, fascinating book about Air Force investigations handled from 1947 to 1955. It was published in 1956 under the title *The Report on Unidentified Flying Objects*. The books by Captain Ruppelt and Lieutenant Colonel Tacker were the basic sources used in gathering information for this and later chapters.

In the Ruppelt book we learn that from 1948 on, there was disagreement among Air Force officials as to the nature of UFOs. One faction outside of the ATIC staff was willing to accept the possibility that *some* UFOs might be interplanetary spaceships. Another faction took the opposite viewpoint that *all* UFOs were nonsense and should be ignored. The Project Blue Book people held to a middle view of "let's find out."

As early as December 27, 1949, a Public Information Officer at Air Force Headquarters in the Pentagon stated, "The saucers are misinterpretations of various conventional objects, mild hysteria, meteorological phenomena, aberrations, or hoaxes."

This is still the basic Air Force position on the identity of UFOs.

Surely some Air Force officials must have wished that the bothersome UFOs would dry up and fade away. The trouble was they didn't. Year after year they became more numerous, more exasperating, more puzzling. Every year produced at least one big, exciting sighting. The Exeter incident made big headlines in 1965 and 1966. And as recently as January 1967 two teenagers in Detroit received nationwide publicity for photographing a UFO. So it looks as if reports of UFOs are here to stay.

On October 25, 1955, Secretary of the Air Force Donald A. Quarles said, "On the basis of a study we believe that no such object such as popularly described as flying saucers has overflown the United States."

On November 5, 1957, another official Air Force spokesman said that after studying and evaluating UFOs for ten years, "no evidence has been discovered to confirm the existence of so-called flying saucers."

The general public accepted these statements. All but a very few believed there were no such things as flying saucers. They hooted and ridiculed anyone who claimed to have seen one. Only a handful of people pointed out a very obvious contradiction: If the Air Force said flying saucers didn't exist, how come it was spending so much time and money studying them?

Within the next year, on October 6, 1958, the

Air Force said something a little bit different. It announced that no evidence had been gathered to prove flying saucers were interplanetary spaceships. Please note: It no longer stated they didn't exist. It said they were not visitors from outer space. On December 24, 1959, the Air Force Inspector General's brief made very clear what the Air Force attitude toward UFOs must be. It declared, "Unidentified Flying Objects — sometimes treated lightly by the press and referred to as 'flying saucers' — must be rapidly and accurately identified as serious Air Force business." Why? Because, the brief said, "UFOs are vitally involved in the Air Force's air-defense mission."

Two and a half years later the Air Force issued regulations privately to its personnel in which it described what UFOs were, why the Air Force remained interested in them, and exactly how a reported sighting must be handled. This official regulation, numbered #202-2 and issued July 20, 1962, described UFOs as being "any aerial phenomena, airborne objects, or objects which are unknown or appear out of the ordinary to the observer because of performance, aerodynamic characteristics, or unusual features."

This same regulation also stated, "Air Force interest in UFOs is threefold. First, as a possible threat to the security of the United States; second, to determine the technical or scientific characteristics of any such UFOs; third, to explain or identify all UFO sightings."

In 1963 the Air Force issued a pamphlet designed to answer some of the questions which civilians ask about Air Force activities. It was entitled *Questions and Answers about the United*

States Air Force. One question included was, "Are there really flying saucers?"

The answer given was, "The term 'flying saucer' is really a science fiction term that was coined several years ago. No unidentified flying object has given any indication of threat to the national security; there has been no evidence submitted to or discovered by the Air Force that unidentified sightings represented technological developments or principles beyond the range of our present scientific knowledge; and finally, there has been nothing in the way of evidence of other data to indicate that these unidentified sightings are extraterrestrial vehicles under intelligent control."

The pamphlet also assured us that "as the Service primarily responsible for aerospace defense, the Air Force will continue to apply the services of its highly qualified scientists and technicians to the task of continuous investigation of all reports of unusual objects over the United States."

In practice the Air Force has never investigated *all* UFO sightings. The task would be impossibly large, would require hundreds of experts and huge sums of money, and would produce much duplicate information.

The most recent and widely read statement of the Air Force position appeared in an article by correspondent Bill Wise in the April 1, 1966, issue of *Life* magazine. It contains an interview with the present head of Project Blue Book, Major Hector Quintanella, Jr., reaffirming the basic Air Force position stated earlier.

Major Quintanella is quoted in this article as saying, "We are spending millions to develop our own rocket boosters to get our spacecraft to the moon and beyond. Imagine what a great help it would be to get our hands on a ship from another planet and examine its power plant." Although not one shred of evidence has turned up to prove UFOs come from outer space, Major Quintanella added, "It is impossible to prove that flying saucers do not exist." This, then, is what the Air Force says about UFOs. What does it *do* about them?

First, of course, someone has to see the UFO. Usually he or she gets excited and races to tell someone else. This can be family, a friend, a law officer, a newspaper, a radio or television station, an airport traffic control crew, or someone connected with the Air Force. One way or another, the word reaches the nearest air base. It is directed to the UFO officer. There is one stationed at every Air Force base in the country.

(Remember, Norman Muscarello at Exeter reported his sighting to the police; they corroborated it and passed on the news to Pease Air Force Base nearby.)

Now regulation #202-2 goes into effect. The rules laid down are rigid, and no one in the Air Force may act contrary to them.

The air base commander, through the UFO officer and his assistants, must then "conduct all investigative action necessary to submit a complete initial report of a UFO sighting. The initial investigation will include every effort to resolve the sighting." After that is done, the air base commander must report directly to the Foreign Technology Division, called FTD, of the Air Force Systems Command at Wright-Patterson Air Force

Base. (FTD has absorbed the Air Technical Intelligence Center.) Next FTD refers the information to Project Blue Book.

Now the very small staff of Project Blue Book goes to work. Major Quintanella, a desk sergeant, and a clerk study the information. They check with other government agencies which deal with weather, radar, balloons, and civilian and military air traffic. They may contact Spacetrack, a project of the National Space Surveillance Control Center located at Bedford, Massachusetts. Spacetrack keeps exact track of the paths of all satellites launched by the United States and Russia. If necessary, Major Quintanella also checks with astronomers, physicists, and other scientists studying aerial phenomena.

After Project Blue Book reaches a decision as to the identity of this particular UFO, it sends a report to the FTD, which forwards it to Air Force Headquarters at the Pentagon. There the data is reviewed by more officers. Then the explanation, or statement, of the official Air Force finding is released by the Office of Information in the Office of the Secretary of the Air Force.

Regulation #202-2 includes one exception to this. The air base commander or the officer in charge of Project Blue Book may "release information to the press or the general public only after positive identification of the sighting as a familiar or known object." Air Force personnel are not allowed to act on their own. The regulation states that they "will not contact private individuals on UFO cases nor will they discuss their operations and function with unauthorized persons unless so directed, and then only on a 'need-to-know' basis."

Sometimes an Air Force spokesman has ridiculed the people involved in a sighting and dismissed it as a wild imagining or a hoax. Sometimes such verdicts are justified. Without exception, whenever one sighting is reported, it triggers a flood of fanciful claims, many of them wholly imagined by crackpots or people who crave publicity. There have been numerous hoaxes, deliberately planned and carried out by people who hoped to make money by selling their story to some gullible newspaper or magazine editor. For instance, there are individuals who claim to have talked with creatures from outer space, been invited aboard spaceships and flown to other planets and back, and had frequent contacts with space dwellers, although they can produce no evidence at all to back up their stories when challenged. It is these people — the so-called crackpot fringe, the publicity hounds, and the hoaxers — who have damaged the serious inquiry into UFOs. They also have prevented reliable, intelligent people from speaking out about the UFOs they have sighted, because they do not want to be labeled liars or mental cases.

From 1947 until 1956 the Air Force was the only important agency investigating UFOs. A few individuals made private inquiries, but their efforts were small and relatively unimportant. However, during this same period, dissatisfaction, first with Air Force official statements and later with the conduct of its investigations, became widespread. A number of sincere, responsible people became convinced that the Air Force knew the truth about UFOs but was deliberately withholding the information on the excuse that the public would panic if it knew the truth. Thus it was inevitable that those who were dissatisfied with the Air Force inquiry into UFOs felt the need for an independent, nongovernment, nonmilitary investigating agency. As a result, in 1956, a number of men, some of them retired military officers, scientists, engineers, and aviation specialists, formed the National Investigations Commission on Aerial Phenomena as described in Chapter 2. Thanks to NICAP, public inquiry into the nature of UFOs has expanded greatly.

The NICAP story follows.

4

The NICAP Position

THE PURPOSE OF NICAP is threefold: one, to investigate all aspects of UFOs; two, to weed out worthless information coming from crackpots and publicity seekers; three, to publicize reliable data received from pilots, scientists, radar technicians, and responsible citizens whose observations cannot simply be dismissed as wild imaginings. For its director and spokesman the founders of NICAP chose Major Donald E. Keyhoe, a retired officer of the U. S. Marine Corps. Two years later an assistant director was added to the staff. In addition, NICAP has special technical advisors drawn from the ranks of rocket and space experts, aeronautical engineers, astronomers, electronics experts, military, commercial, and private pilots, congressmen, government officials, newspapermen, doctors, lawyers, teachers, ministers, and other educated, responsible citizens.

NICAP worked hard to correct the mistaken impressions many people had acquired from the wild and unbelievable tales told by crackpots and hoaxers. Its directors felt there should be some agency to which responsible people could report sightings without fear of being ridiculed. Also, since the United States was making tremendous strides in space exploration and space-vehicle design, the directors felt that it was possible that more advanced civilizations could exist on other planets and could send spaceships to study what is happening on our planet Earth.

Members of NICAP now number over 10,000 and live in all fifty states and thirty foreign countries. They pay modest annual dues which help defray the expenses of the director and his assistant, and the clerical help and offices maintained in Washington, D.C. Every two months NICAP publishes a newsletter called *The U.F.O. Investigator*. This carries reports on very recent UFO sightings made by NICAP volunteer investigators.

In 1964 NICAP published a 184-page casebook crammed with the information it had gathered on 746 UFO sightings. An extra 171 cases were included in tables which showed where most UFO sightings have been made. This casebook, entitled *The UFO Evidence,* classified each sighting as to date, place, kind of object seen, and additional brief facts describing the sighting. Then each sighting was listed in separate chapters which dealt with observations made by Air Force personnel, by other Armed Services people, by pilots and aviation experts, by scientists and engineers, and by lawmen and everyday citizens. It also included a digest of the general features of UFO reports; special evidence such as electromagnetic effects, radar cases, and photographic evidence; some foreign sightings; patterns of sightings; and a chronological list of American sightings. There were charts, maps, and sketches too.

The author has used *The UFO Evidence* as the principal source for presenting NICAP findings on various UFO sightings which occurred up to 1964. *The U.F.O. Investigator* was the source for NICAP inquiries into sightings occurring between 1964 and 1967.

From the day it was founded in 1956, NICAP has criticized the Air Force for saying on the one hand that UFOs were serious business, but on the other hand that they could be dismissed as nonsense. There must have been some jusitification for this criticism, because even Captain Ruppelt suggests in his book that about 1955 there were definite indications of a movement within the Air Force to "write them all off, regardless" — in spite of numerous convincing radar-visual sightings. Captain Ruppelt wrote, "When a ground radar picks up a UFO target and a ground observer sees a light where the radar target is located, then a jet interceptor is scrambled [sent] to intercept the UFO and the pilot also sees the light and gets a radar lock on, only to have the UFO almost impudently outdistance him, there is no simple answer."

Of course, the Air Force wants to reduce the number of unexplained sightings to zero, but to "write them all off, regardless" is not the way to arrive at the truth. Yet, in spite of the increasing need for the right kind of information, the Air Force has cut back the thoroughness and scope of its investigations. By 1965, for example, the Project Blue Book staff had been reduced to one officer and two assistants. Meantime NICAP has been trying to fill this gap by examining as many UFO sightings as possible and making the information available for study.

How does NICAP become involved in a UFO sighting? In two ways, apparently: one, from firsthand observations supplied by members and, two, from newspaper or magazine articles sent by members to headquarters. The actual investigations are carried out by volunteer subcommittees or field units made up of specially trained or equipped personnel. NICAP openly disagrees with the Air Force position that, given the right kind of information, all UFOs can be identified as real objects or known aerial phenomenon. It rejects the flat statement that there are no such things as UFOs originating in outer space. The NICAP position is that *some* UFOs could be spaceships or other objects not originating on earth.

NICAP has helped greatly to distribute information about our country's frequent UFO sightings. It has involved more people in finding out what UFOs might be. Through the numerous books and magazine articles which Major Keyhoe has written, many Americans have learned more about UFOs than they ever would have from Air Force Public Information.

Now that we have seen the position of the Air Force and NICAP in regard to UFOs, let us get back to the Exeter incident. If you remember, Norman Muscarello and the two patrolmen sighted the UFO early in the morning of September

3, 1965. Later that day two officers from Pease
Air Force Base arrived to make their investigation. They sent their data on to Project Blue
Book. At this point NICAP lent a hand. At about
the same time that writer John Fuller arrived in
Exeter to begin his interviews, Ray Fowler, a
field investigator for NICAP, also began his inquiry. Then on October 27, as we saw in Chapter
1, the Air Force stated officially that the sightings
had been either stars and planets in unusual formations, a high-altitude Strategic Air Command
exercise, or a temperature inversion that caused
stars and planets to twinkle. The people of Exeter, Mr. Fuller, and particularly the two patrolmen rejected these Air Force explanations.

Other surprising notes gathered included "constant radar reports" recorded at the Portsmouth
Navy Base for some months after Norman's original sighting. There a UFO was seen both visually and on radar hovering over the base water
tower. An object landed near one of the runways
at Pease Air Force Base and lighted a wide area.
When a fire unit was dispatched to investigate,
the object streaked off. An Air Force refueling
officer told Mr. Fuller off-the-record that a refueling operation had been broken off abruptly
when an enormous UFO appeared directly off
the wing of a KC-97 tanker. This UFO was seen
by the crew and by a radar technician. Another
night a Coast Guardsman, speaking off-the-record, said he was nearly scared out of his wits
when he saw an enormous red-orange disc move
slowly along the ocean front. On still another
night Exeter residents and Mr. Fuller saw a red-

orange object streak across the sky at incredible speed, with a jet plane in pursuit.

As late as February 1966, people in the Exeter area were still sighting UFOs. On February 9, 1966, a spokesman for the Air Force wrote Patrolman Bertrand and Hunt that "we have been unable to identify the object you observed on September 3, 1965."

Thus the same conclusion — namely, that the UFO was an *unidentified* flying object — had been reached by the Air Force, by John Fuller, and by Mr. Fowler of NICAP. Yet the basic disagreements still existed: The Air Force did not think that the Exeter UFOs could have come from outer space, whereas Mr. Fuller and Mr. Fowler suggested that they could.

One may well ask, "Didn't anyone make a scientific examination of the evidence?" The answer is yes.

An electrical engineer who specialized in aerial phenomena studied the statements, the weather conditions, and other technical information. The man was Philip J. Klass, who also is Editor of *Aviation Week* magazine and holds a B.S. degree from Iowa State University. He concluded that one strong clue to the explanation of the UFOs was the fact that some of the sightings were made very close to high-tension power lines and, therefore, may only have been electricity-generated lightning. He stated his conclusion in an article entitled "Plasma Theory May Explain Many UFOs," which was published in the April 22, 1966, issue of *Aviation Week & Space Technology*.

Mr. Klass wrote, "A special form of ball lightning generated by electric corona that occurs on high-tension power lines under certain conditions may explain many sightings of lower altitude unidentified flying objects." He said there was a striking similarity between the reported characteristics of ball lightning and the UFOs sighted by dozens of persons in the Exeter area. Mr. Klass described ball lightning as normally either spherical or ellipsoidal, doughnut- or ring-shaped. It can be multicolored but is usually red or less frequently intense bluish-white or green. It can hang motionless at times, zip about at high speeds, roll, glide, and spin. It can be visible for periods from a few seconds to many minutes. So, as a result of his study, Mr. Klass reached the conclusion that the Exeter UFO sightings were caused by "ball lightning."

But Mr. Fuller pointed out that while the ball-lightning possibility might apply to some of the many Exeter sightings, it could not be accepted as the only answer for two reasons. First, so far ball lightning has not been observed as being larger in size than a grapefruit, and, second, too many of the Exeter sightings refer to a huge *structured* craft, not small globs of light.

Who was right? It is impossible to say. No adequate photographs exist, no "hardware" or material evidence was gathered. All the answers were based on educated guesses. It looks as if neither the Air Force, NICAP, Mr. Fuller, nor Mr. Klass has produced a complete, satisfactory answer.

5

Some Famous Incidents

1. *The Mantell Crash*

SINCE 1948 the Air Force has scored many successes in solving the mystery surrounding many UFO sightings. A few cases gained such nationwide attention that in time they were considered "classic cases." They stand out as examples of exciting sightings which were solved when enough of the right kind of information was gathered. One of these was the Mantell crash.

The incident began the afternoon of January 7, 1948, when lights on the switchboard at the Kentucky State Highway Patrol Office in Frankfort flashed repeatedly. The office received call after call from persons who had spotted a strange object in the sky.

"What does it look like?" the officer on duty asked each caller.

Each said the object was huge, maybe three hundred feet in diameter, and round. It was

moving westward across Kentucky. Since it seemed headed for Fort Knox, where the U. S. Gold
Depository containing the nation's gold supply is
located, the officer alerted Godman Air Force
Base close by. There, the men on duty in the air
traffic control tower immediately scanned the
sky with binoculars.

After an intense watch, one of the crew exclaimed, "I see it! Man, is it big! It's shaped like
a tear drop!"

"More like an ice cream cone," another said.

A third observer noticed the immense metallic
object was rose-colored on top, probably from the
sun's reflection. "What do you suppose it is?"

The crew chief reached for the telephone. "I
better call the C.O."

The C.O., or Commanding Officer, was Colonel Guy Hix. He and his aide rushed to the
tower. They, too, saw the object.

At that moment, 2:30 P.M., a flight of four
National Guard F-51 Mustang aircraft came in
sight to the south. The flight leader radioed his
position. He was Captain Thomas Mantell. He
explained that the four planes were being ferried
from Georgia to an air base near Louisville.

"Tell the captain to investigate the object,"
Colonel Hix ordered.

The tower operator contacted Mantell. "Say,
there's an object south of here that we can't
identify. Have you enough gas to take a look at
it for us?"

Mantell answered, "Roger. Give me the heading on it."

After furnishing the information, the operator
left open the speaker. He and the others heard

the captain contact his wing pilots. One of his wing pilots reported that he was short on fuel, and was told to fly on to Louisville. The other two pilots agreed to follow Mantell's lead.

At 2:45 P.M. Mantell radioed in, "Altitude 15,000 feet. I have an object in sight above and ahead of me. I'd say it was moving at about half my speed, or about 180 miles an hour."

The tower operator said, "Describe the object."

Although static made it difficult to hear Mantell clearly, he is supposed to have reported seeing a metallic object of tremendous size. "I'm going up to 20,000 for a better look."

Each of the two remaining wing pilots reported, "I can see the object with Mantell following close behind." It must be added here that none of the three pilots had oxygen masks with them. At that moment one of the two wing pilots reported he was running short of fuel and was told to proceed to Louisville. The remaining wing pilot landed, took on fuel and an oxygen mask, and again took to the air.

Meanwhile Captain Mantell reported, "20,000 feet. Still climbing. I'll go up to 25,000, stay ten minutes, and then come in. Over."

Colonel Hix was worried. "Mantell should not go that high without an oxygen mask. Tell him to discontinue the search."

The tower operator called Mantell on the radio. No answer was heard through the static. He tried again, and again. Meantime all in the tower had lost sight of him and the UFO in their glasses.

Slightly before 3:15 Mantell's voice came through clearly. "The object is directly ahead of me. Slightly above. Moving at my speed or better. I'm trying to close in for a better look."

That was the last anyone ever heard from Captain Thomas Mantell. After an anxious period when the pilot did not return, Colonel Hix ordered another plane out to investigate. "I'm going to my office. Keep me posted." He and his aide left.

The crew kept watch. About an hour later the pilot sent out to look for Mantell radioed, "I have spotted some wreckage below." He gave the exact location.

Men from the air base and State Police sped to the crash. A crowd gathered. Several bystanders had seen the UFO. They asked the air base men if the UFO had had anything to do with the crash. The men admitted that the F-51 had been dispatched to pursue the UFO.

People began talking excitedly. Many jumped to the conclusion that the dead pilot had gotten too close to the mysterious object and had been destroyed by some strange weapon. The talk grew wilder and wilder. Then when the pilot's body was pried from the wreckage, some one close by shouted, "His body is full of bullet holes!"

The word spread throughout the crowd, giving rise to still more rumors. Reporters wrote these down and later included them in their stories. As a result, a good many people throughout the country sincerely believed a mysterious spacecraft, either from Russia or from outer space, had blown Mantell's plane to bits with some strange weapon.

Meantime a painstaking investigation of the wreckage was begun by government aviation crash experts and an officer from the Air Technical Intelligence Center. These men found that the pilot's watch had stopped at 3:18 P.M. and that his body was not riddled with bullet holes. The plane had not burned, and the crumpled fuselage was not radioactive.

Perhaps this is the place to note that, although there has been much talk about comic strip "death rays" and radioactive beams, there is no foundation for or proof of a dangerous radiation hazard accompanying the appearance of UFOs.

After further lengthy examination of the wreckage of the F-51, the investigators decided that Captain Mantell had flown too high and lost unconsciousness from lack of oxygen. Without the pilot's hands on the controls, the plane had leveled off. Then, because of engine torque, it began to turn gradually and went into a spiraling dive. A wing tore off, and then came the crash.

But the big question remained: What was the mysterious object Mantell had been pursuing?

Among the data that the ATIC man had picked up at the scene of the crash was the possibility that tht pilot actually had seen the planet Venus instead of a real object closer to him. The ATIC man checked and found out Venus was in such a position in the sky that it could have been seen by the pilot. Later he reported this to the Pentagon, and the Public Officer speedily put out the explanation that the pilot had been confused by the planet Venus, had flown too high without oxygen, and had, therefore, crashed.

Flying-saucer fans scoffed at the idea and dug up evidence which contradicted this. They learned from astronomers that the chances of Captain

Mantell's seeing Venus were very slight because at that time of day the planet would have appeared no larger than a small pinpoint of light. Meanwhile the log of the conversation between the tower and the pilot showed he had reported sighting an object that was huge and metallic.

Naturally the dead pilot's family was very much upset, not only by their tragic loss, but by the disturbing rumors. However, since it could be proved the pilot had no oxygen mask and had himself reported he intended to fly to 25,000 feet, which is exceedingly dangerous to attempt without the use of oxygen, there was little doubt as to how and why the crash had occurred. It seemed as if this were all that would ever be known.

But in 1952, four years after the crash, some new and formerly secret information was made public. This news described a project in which the Navy launched what it called Skyhook balloons to obtain high-altitude information about winds and cosmic rays. The Skyhook balloons were huge and in flight looked like gigantic tear drops. They carried many scientific instruments. Their course was determined by the winds. Thus they could change directions and speeds, according to the winds they encountered. Because the sunlight reflected off their surfaces, they could be seen from the ground even when 60,000 feet high. If they flew too high, they burst, and the pieces scattered. If they developed a leak, they changed shape and fell to earth.

When Captain Ruppelt, then in charge of Project Blue Book, read about these huge balloons, he did some checking. He learned that some of the balloons had been launched from Clinton

County Air Force Base in southern Ohio, and the path of one had been charted across Kentucky. This rang a bell in his mind, and he studied the data on the Mantell crash. The appearance of the UFO reported that day matched that of a Skyhook balloon. With this new and exciting clue, he worked incessantly to learn more about the launchings. Yes, one had been launched the day the F-51 had crashed. He cross-checked weather reports and made sure the balloon would have blown along a path which made it visible at Godman Air Force Base at the approximate time the UFO was sighted. When the major points matched, Captain Ruppelt heaved a great sigh of relief. At last the identity of the mysterious UFO was known. Undoubtedly it was a Skyhook balloon. Since it soared many thousands of feet higher than an F-51 could fly, Captain Mantell never could have closed in on it, even if he had been wearing an oxygen mask.

Captain Ruppelt placed the folder of data on the Mantell crash in the file of those which Project Blue Book labeled as solved, or *Known*. He passed the new information on to the pilot's family, who were much relieved to hear it. He also sent the information to the Pentagon. But because the crash *had* occurred so long before, the Public Information Officer did not publicize the new findings. The truth was not widely known until Captain Ruppelt's book was published.

The Mantell case is important because it shows how, when the right kind of information is available, a UFO can be identified as a real or known object.

2. *A V-Formation of Lights*

Ever since 1948 many of the UFOs sighted have been described as bright lights zipping about the night sky. Usually they are seen for only a few seconds and, therefore, are almost impossible to identify. However, the Air Technical Intelligence Center people have identified a number of these by dint of much hard digging for facts. In his book Lieutenant Colonel Tacker devoted an entire chapter to showing how easy it is to be fooled and to mistake perfectly ordinary aircraft for UFOs.

Briefly, what kinds of objects or aerial phenomena do observers mistake for UFOs?

Many are very bright stars or planets or meteors. Others are satellites. Some are large balloons released by weather stations, airports, and research studies. Some are everyday aircraft. On occasion, unidentified blips seen on radar screens are the result of mechanical malfunctions or interference from other electronic devices.

In the *Life* article mentioned in Chapter 3, author Wise stated, "There is no question that our Air Force and those of other countries employ assorted airborne hardware as tactical and training devices. Many of these are, of course, 'seen' as flying saucers and it is obvious that for security reasons the Air Force is reluctant to talk about them."

In other words, the United States and other countries now have secret "airborne hardware" which they are not going to describe as long as secrecy is important to the country's defense. Furthermore, many sightings are so unexpected, and usually so brief, and cause the observers to get so excited, that often the wrong impression is gained.

A good example of this occurred the night of October 8, 1954, in southern California. Hundreds of people in and around the Los Angeles area watched a V-formation of lights move soundlessly across the sky. Many dashed to report their presence. Switchboards at airports, radio stations, police stations, and sheriffs' offices lighted up as calls poured in from every direction. Pilots approaching or departing from the Los Angeles airport confirmed the sightings. Some observers excitedly swore they had seen flying saucers or discs even though it was nighttime. However, most people, including the pilots, reported seeing only lights. Naturally the reports were relayed to various Air Force bases. Intelligence officers immediately started checking and inside an hour had the full and correct story.

3. *Pacific Fireball*

At 3:00 A.M. Honolulu time on July 12, 1959, Pan American Airways Flight #947 from San Francisco was well out over the Pacific Ocean. In four hours it would set down at Honolulu International Airport. A few moments earlier the pilot, Captain C. A. Wilson, had radioed in his position. All was well aboard. It was a star-bright night, and the air was calm. The passengers were reading or dozing, the stewardesses relaxing. This was just another routine safe flight across the water.

Captain Wilson glanced at his copilot, Richard Lorenzon, who was watching the lighted instrument panel on the Boeing Stratocruiser. "All instruments green," Lorenzon said.

As the captain did hundreds of times on each flight, he looked out the window to his left. Below he could see a sheen reflecting off the ocean. Above, the stars were brilliant in a clear sky.

Suddenly the picture changed. A cluster of white lights appeared with stunning swiftness and sped across the heavens toward the airliner at a fantastic rate of speed. Pilot, copilot and flight engineer watched them for at least ten seconds. Then, without slowing down, the lights made a sharp right turn and disappeared.

"What was that?" the copilot exclaimed.

"It's no meteor, that's for sure," the pilot said. All agreed the object could not have been a plane. The pilot switched on the radio and contacted the Honolulu Radio Control Center. "Pan American Flight nine four seven," he reported.

The Air Traffic Controller at Honolulu answered immediately, "We read you."

Captain Wilson reported the plane's position. "We are 28 degrees, 25 minutes North; 144 degrees, 30 minutes West. Altitude 20,000 feet. We have just sighted bright white lights moving at a high speed in a generally eastern direction. These appeared to be one bright center light with four smaller lights on the left side. The object moved approximately 180 degrees to our flight path and made a 90-degree turn. Lights slightly higher in altitude than aircraft. Objects verified by two other crew members. End of message."

Although his heart was thumping, the captain

grinned at his crew. "Want to bet we're in for some questions when we set down in Honolulu?"

The other two nodded. Each returned to his important task, and the flight continued without further incident.

Meanwhile the receiver at Air Traffic Control Headquarters in Honolulu was crackling with other messages. Even though the pilots tried to report in their usual matter-of-fact manner, there was suppressed excitement in their voices.

The second call came in from Captain E. G. Mathwig of Pan American Airways Flight #942. He had seen the light too. "It could be a shooting star. The sighting lasted ten to fifteen seconds."

Another report came in from Captain Zedwick of Slick Airways Flight #719. He said the lights appeared to be only a mile away. "The object appeared to be one large light, with four smaller lights in the trail. It came right at us. Flight path seemed level with our aircraft and speed very high. It could have been a meteor."

Then Empress Flight #223 checked in, reporting the strange object as one large light surrounded by a cluster of six or seven smaller lights. All were moving faster than known aircraft. But Captain L. C. Moffat stated, "Object definitely not a meteor or shooting star. No trail visible."

The pilot of United Airlines Flight #21 said, "Have just sighted white light dead ahead and above aircraft. It descended toward aircraft and went below, then banked to left. As the object moved away, there were four white lights in a rectangle with a large bright light in the center. End of report."

Four more flights added their information: Pan American #752 and #945, Canadian Pacific #323 and Slick #601. The reports were similar.

On the ground at Honolulu the Chief Air Control Officer told his crew hastily, "Verify those reports." He grabbed the telephone. He alerted officers on duty at the headquarters of the Western Sea Frontier, which coordinates defense of the Pacific. Then he called the Pacific Air Force, and the office of its commander-in-chief. After a hasty conference Pacific Air Force said they would not dispatch aircraft to investigate the lights because the sightings were too far out of range.

One by one the airliners came in for routine landings. Their crews signed out. Military intelligence men drew pilots and copilots into a private room for questioning. Newspapermen were present. Captain Wilson made the first statement: "My copilot and flight engineer both saw the bright light as it came toward us at an extremely high rate of speed. For at least ten seconds it maintained its course, which was on an opposite heading to us. Had it been another aircraft, it would have passed well to our left. Suddenly the object made a sharp right turn at a speed inconceivable for any vehicle we know of, and the light suddenly disappeared. The smaller lights were evenly spaced, and were either part of the mysterious object, or this was an example of darn good formation flying."

One reporter interrupted. "How long have you been flying, sir?"

"Nineteen years," Captain Wilson answered.

"Have you ever seen anything like this before?"

"Never."

Half jokingly, the reporter said, "Could it have been one of those flying saucers?"

The pilot pinned down the reporter with a steady look. "I have never believed such foreign objects existed." Then he took a deep breath. "I'm a believer now."

The other airmen offered similar reports. Although admittedly concerned, the intelligence officers were happy about one thing. Never before had so many almost identical detailed reports come in from so many well-qualified observers flying over such a broad area.

After the airmen were dismissed, the newspapermen dashed for telephones. Soon radio, teletype, and telephone messages were flashing across the Pacific to the mainland. Newspapers hit the streets with extra headlining: PILOTS REPORT UNIDENTIFIED FLYING OBJECT.

Telephones jangled at the Pentagon as excited citizens called in to learn what it was the pilots had seen. All the Air Force spokesman could say was that the matter was being investigated, and a report would be made later.

Project Blue Book staff went to work. They examined each pilot's statement. They gathered all the weather data for the sighting area. On a map they charted the position of each aircraft in relation to the unidentified lights. They checked to see if any satellites or balloons had been aloft. None had. They checked the position of the moon and stars. Gradually the evidence pointed to one, and only one answer: The bright light had come from a fireball.

A fireball is a meteor which is exceptionally brilliant. Its color can range from blue-white to yellow to red. Many have been seen, and the sight is always the same: a sudden brilliant flash of light which lasts as long as the meteor is visible. Sometimes the fireball breaks into several parts and appears to be several lights. A fireball need not necessarily leave a fiery trail behind it as other meteors do. The light fades as quickly as it comes. From data obtained by previous checks on fireballs it appears that their speed can reach as high as 100,000 miles per hour.

Thanks to the map drawn and the fact that the time, description, and general direction of the bright lights were so similar, the verdict was soon forthcoming: The object all had seen was a fireball. All the pilots and copilots accepted this decision, even Captain Wilson, who was quite relieved!

Project Blue Book labeled this sighting as solved, or *Known*.

Since the pilots and their crews soon took off on other flights, they were not available for questioning by anyone representing NICAP. In its casebook *The UFO Evidence,* NICAP included the sightings in a chronological list but made no mention of the answer provided by the Air Force.

4. *Dying Satellites*

A more recent sighting that caused considerable excitement occurred after midnight on April 8,

1964. A large and very brilliant bluish-white light was spotted by civilian and military observers in Connecticut. Its speed was unbelievable. Suddenly the UFO changed color to red. Smaller objects detached themselves from the main body and trailed behind. As it was tracked southward, air control towers at airports and defense installations all the way to Long Island began to receive reports on it. In every case, the details were similar. So many calls were received that one air base officer joked, "There must be a heck of a lot of people along the East Coast who don't go to bed early."

Only a few moments later reports were being radioed from ships cruising about the Caribbean Sea. But now the details varied. Some described a flaming object with a long tapered tail, or a flaming red or green ball followed by smaller objects, or a light with a trail which resembled a peacock's tail, or a blue-white fireball with an orange tail. Observers on one vessel claimed the light radiating from the UFO was so brilliant that the deck and surrounding waters were flooded with light. Another stated that the main object exploded into fifteen fragments, and these fell into a formation and streaked out of sight. The captain of an oil tanker saw an object that was round and blue-white on top, but flattened and red below, and was giving off sparks.

Next people in the Virgin Islands began to see the mysterious object. Some were frightened by it. One native swore he saw a big green globe which was followed by a flaming cigar-shaped object. Others insisted there were two lighted objects followed by a cluster of small ones. All disappeared into a cloud bank.

The last sightings came from the coast of British Guiana where a red object cut a flaming swath across the sky and dropped from sight into the Atlantic Ocean.

The northernmost sightings were reported to East Coast newspapers and appeared the next day as news items. One alert UFO-minded reporter jotted down the location of the sightings and came up with the startling news that all were in a straight north-to-south line. He also noted all had been seen within a period of five minutes. Therefore, the reporter figured, it was reasonable to guess all were of the same object. The article he wrote revealed these facts, and more; namely, that the object seen was absolutely silent, had not looked like a meteor, and had appeared to be traveling about 16,000 miles per hour. He left it up to the readers to decide what the far-ranging UFO really was.

Apparently there were a great many readers who felt they knew what it was. They swamped the poor reporter with telephone calls, insisting the object was either a fleet of spaceships invading earth, or a "mother" ship dispatching smaller discs to spy on our Army and Navy installations! One astronomer reported that the lights were positively meteors.

Meanwhile the details of the sightings had reached Project Blue Book. After a quick analysis the officer in charge placed a telephone call to the National Space Surveillance Control Center at Bedford, Massachusetts. Its project Spacetrack was able to provide the correct answer to the long-range sightings. Spacetrack technicians said that what the observers had watched over Russia's Sputnik II, launched November 3, 1957, plunging to a fiery death as it came down through the earth's atmosphere.

The Air Force lost no time in making public the facts about this *identified* flying object.

A similar sighting which produced another flood of telephone calls across the country began on March 7, 1960. About 8 P.M. that evening, reports began to come in from observers who lived close to Lake Erie. They had sighted a brilliant object flashing across the heavens. Additional sightings were reported all the way south to Miami, Florida.

Project Blue Book contacted Spacetrack and learned that people had seen the satellite Discoverer VIII reentering the earth's atmosphere and breaking up. Once more sky watchers had seen the death of a satellite, and the Air Force could label another sighting as *Known*.

By showing you the ways in which Air Force investigations are conducted, we have tried to give you an idea of how Project Blue Book does look into sightings.

Now you can see how easy it is to be fooled, and how the air traffic, weather, and aerial phenomena of a given date and time can be checked to provide clues leading to the real identities of some UFOs. These incidents also help point out that when enough of the right kind of information is available, a UFO can often be identified satisfactorily.

6

The Scoutmaster
and the Strange Light

SINCE THE FLYING-SAUCER CRAZE began twenty
years ago, the United States Air Force Project
Blue Book has investigated almost twelve thousand sightings of unidentified flying objects. Most
of these were reported by responsible people.
However, from time to time, someone deliberately
plans a faked sighting in order to gain publicity or
money. Some go so far as to fake photographs of
flying saucers by throwing a hubcap or a bottle cap
high in the air, and photographing it. These attempts usually fail because experts can analyze a
photograph and tell whether it has been
"arranged." Other individuals have photographed
a dummy clad in silver-colored coveralls, with the
face covered, and claimed this was a man from
outer space whose body was taken from a spaceship that had crashed. But when reporters and
NICAP investigators demand to see the creature
and his spaceship, the hoaxers claimed the Air
Force had spirited both away!

Other people have told newsmen that they have talked with creatures from outer space and have ridden in their spaceships to Mars and back.

"Didn't you need a pressurized suit and oxygen mask?" the newsmen asked.

"Oh, no," these people claimed airily, though even children know about the suits and gear our astronauts must use in the orbits around the earth.

There are numerous clubs about the country where people gather to tell about their space flights and space conversations. There are magazines which print these stories as if they were the truth, and not out and out fabrications. One of the most famous hoaxes was perpetrated by a scoutmaster. The story follows.

The evening of August 19, 1952, at West Palm Beach, Florida, a scoutmaster whom we shall call Mr. Smith brought his troop meeting to a close. Most of the boys poured out of the hall, jumped on their bicycles, and rode off. One lad looked a little downcast.

"What's the matter, Johnny? Don't you have a ride home?" Mr. Smith asked.

"Naw, my bike's got a flat tire. I got to walk."

The scoutmaster thought quickly. Johnny lived nearly three miles from the meeting hall. None of the other scouts lived in his direction. He would have to walk a dark country road alone. "I don't want you walking that road alone even if it is only nine-thirty. I'll drive you home. And you too, fellows," he said to three others who were without bikes.

The five piled into Smith's car and drove along a graveled country road bordered with a thick growth of palmetto and scrub pine.

"Those woods are sure dark, aren't they?" Mr. Smith remarked.

The boys agreed. "They're full of poisonous snakes, too," Johnny added.

"My dad says there's a wild cat prowling around there," another boy remarked. "He heard it scream the night he was out hunting raccoons."

"Y'all ever hear a hooty owl in the woods at night?" the third boy asked. "That's the spookiest-sounding bird I know."

The scoutmaster spoke up. "Say, have you boys read about the flying saucers that have been seen around these parts? A dark woods like this would be a perfect place for one of them to hide."

The boys agreed again a little shakily. Just the thought of mysterious spaceships invading the earth made them shiver. One had been reported by an airline pilot flying off the Florida coast recently. The boys had talked a great deal about it at the time. They were sure it was a spaceship from Mars or the moon.

Johnny laughed nervously. "If I saw one of those things, I'd be scared stiff."

"I'd run in the house and get my dad's rifle, and shoot it."

"I'd call the police."

"I'd run for cover."

Mr. Smith stopped the talk. "Let's not get carried away, boys. Chances of our seeing a flying saucer in this part of the country are mighty slim."

The talk switched to whether the boys would have an overnight camp-out at the beach before school started. Mr. Smith listened with half an ear as he watched the unlighted road. There was no traffic on it even at this early evening hour.

Some time later he braked hard.

"What's the matter?" all the boys asked.

Smith's voice was tight. "I swear I saw a light flickering behind those trees!" He turned to Johnny, who was in the back seat. "There are no houses along this stretch, are there, Johnny?"

Johnny shook his head. "Nope."

The light flickered again at treetop level.

"There it is!" the boys chorused.

Smith stopped the car, turned off the ignition, and doused his headlights. "I don't like it. I'm going to investigate." He rummaged in a glove compartment and brought out two flashlights. He put one in his back pants pocket. Then he pulled a machete from under the car seat.

"Hey, what are you going to do with that?"

"I'm taking it, just in case," Mr. Smith said. "Now, look here, boys. Y'all stay in the car. There's no telling what is causing those lights. If I'm not back in fifteen minutes, you go for help, hear?"

"Yes, sir!" All were a little frightened, and didn't argue about having to stay in the car.

With eyes wide, they watched Smith's flashlight flickering as he went through the brush into the woods.

They waited and waited. After what seemed like an hour had passed and Smith had not returned, they were very nervous.

"I think we ought to go for help," Johnny said.

"Me, too. But I'm not walking back down that dark road alone."

"We could all go."

"Yeah, let's. I think something awful has happened to Mr. Smith."

The four ran back down the road until they were out of breath. Then they dog-trotted until they came to a house.

A man answered their knock on the door. After they had explained their errand, he asked, "Is this a joke, boys, or are you on the level?"

"On the level, Scout's honor," they all said at once.

The man called the sheriff's office. Soon after a patrol car drove up. In it were a constable and a deputy. Once more the boys explained.

"Pile in back," the constable said. "We'll drive out and have a look."

On arriving at the scene, they saw Smith's car. The constable drew off to the side of the road behind it. He and the deputy stepped out, flashlights in hand. "You boys want to come with us, or stay in the car?"

The boys eyed one another. They guessed nothing would happen to them if the stuck close to the officers.

The constable led the way, the boys at his heels, and the deputy brought up the rear. All moved slowly, looking carefully over the woods revealed in the flashlights' bright beams. They entered a stand of scrub pine. It was as dark as a tunnel. Advancing step by step, they moved farther from the road. Every time a branch brushed them, or they stumbled over a root, the boys held their breaths.

About 150 yards in, the constable stopped.

This weather phenomenon is known to meteorologists as parhelia. Occurring at high altitudes, the bright spots are a refraction of the sun's light.

This type of mirage is often mistaken for flying saucers.

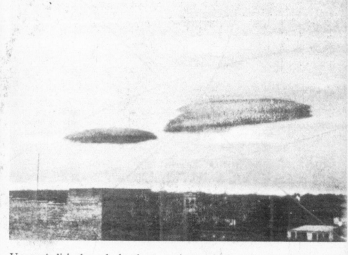

Unusual disk-shaped clouds occurring at high altitudes (called lenticular clouds) are often mistaken for UFOs. U.S. AIR FORCE

These are noctilucent clouds, so called because they are luminous and appear only at night. U.S. AIR FORCE

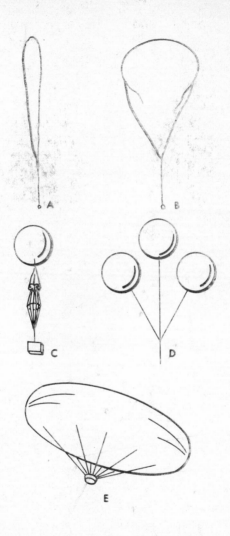

Weather balloons at high altitudes are often mistaken for UFOs.
The balloons shown here are A, Skyhook balloon at launching;
B, Skyhook at high altitude; C, radiosonde or pibal; D, balloon
cluster; and E, blimp or sausage-shaped balloon.

DOUBLEDAY & COMPANY, INC.

Major Hector Quintanilla, Jr., director of the Air Force's Project Blue Book.

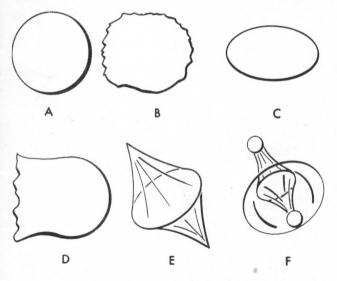

Occasional UFOs will appear on film although they were not visible to the photographer at the time of shooting. These are most often caused by a lens defect in the camera. Above, A is a true image produced by the camera, while B through F are faulty images.

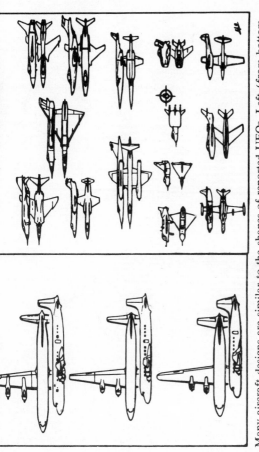

Many aircraft designs are similar to the shapes of reported UFOs. Left (from bottom to top): DC-4, DC-6, and DC-7. Right: top, A-11. Second row, F4F "phantom"; F-106 Delta Dart; F-105 Thunderchief. Third row, F-104 Starfighter; F-101 Voodoo. Fourth row, British T-188 (high-speed research); X-3 Stiletto. Fifth row, British VTOL; X-13; French Coleopter VTOL; XF-85 Goblin. Sixth row, F-94 Starfire; F-84F Thunderstreak; P-59.

NICAP

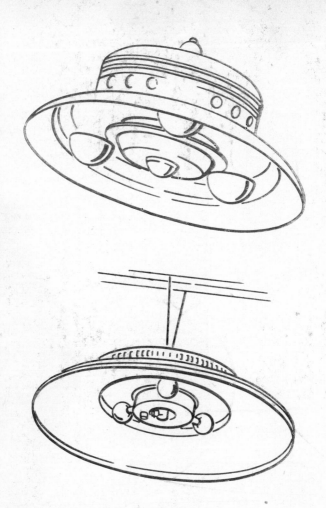

The upper drawing was taken from a photograph of a "space-ship from Venus." The possessor of the photograph also claims to have traveled from Kansas City, Missouri, to Davenport, Iowa, in the ship. It bears a striking resemblance to a chicken brooder, shown in lower drawing. DOUBLEDAY & COMPANY, INC.

This is an aerial photograph of a B-36 jet bomber. Because such bombers appear as thin black disks in photographs, they are often mistaken for UFOs.

U.S. AIR FORCE

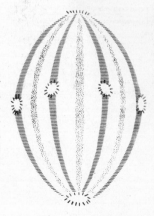

This is a sketch of the planet Jupiter as seen through a jet trail. Passage of the jet caused atmospheric turbulence and temperature change, which in turn caused the refraction of the planet's light into streaks of red, blue, and green, as well as the original yellow.

DOUBLEDAY & COMPANY, INC.

Fifteen-year-old Neil Batey of Clevedon, Somerset, proudly displays the flying saucer he discovered on a nearby hill. The saucer, which emitted a beeping sound, was one of five found scattered throughout southern England in September 1967. Upon examination, its contents were found to include two car batteries, a British-made radio transmitter, a six-inch loudspeaker. It was decided the objects had not come from outer space.   UPI

He switched off his flashlight. "Quiet! I hear something!"

All listened. They strained to see, but could not even make out the shapes of the trees.

"Oh, golly, I'm scared," one boy whimpered.

"Shhhh!"

All was quiet for a moment. Then they heard something. It was a moan.

The constable flicked on his light. He pushed ahead quickly. They heard another moan. It sounded closer. Then the officer stumbled over the body of a man.

"That's Mr. Smith!" the boys exclaimed.

Smith was trying feebly to sit up. The boys took over holding the flashlights while the officers lifted him to his feet. Smith clutched them frantically. "Have they gone?" he cried out, obviously frightened.

"Who? What? What happened?" the men asked.

Smith started to rub his forehead. "Ouch! My hand! The back of my hand is burned!"

Everybody looked. The hair was singed off the back of his right hand.

"What happened?" said the constable again. "Now, y'all take it easy, man, and tell us what happened."

Haltingly, with nervous glances over his shoulder, Smith said, "Well, first, while driving along the road, I saw this mysterious light at tree-top level. It was flickering deep in the woods. I stopped and turned off my headlights so I could see better. The light flashed again. The boys saw it. Didn't you, boys?"

"Yes, sir."

Smith continued. "I had two flashlights and a machete in the car. I took them with me into the woods."

"And we stayed in the car like you told us to," Johnny said.

"One of the first things I noticed was this peculiar smell," Smith went on. "And it was hot, awfully hot, almost like a blast from a furnace. Unnaturally hot. But I kept going toward the light. All at once I looked up, and there was a huge round object hovering over me! No kidding! It had a sort of turretlike dome in the middle, and it blotted out most of the sky.

"Before I could holler or duck, a door opened on this thing. And — now, y'all won't believe this, but so help me, it really happened — a ball of fire popped out, and came right at me! First thing I knew I was all bound up in this ball of fire. Then I — I guess I fainted."

Smith seemed a little embarrassed at admitting he was scared. Everyone understood. It had been a frightening experience.

"I'd like to get home," he continued. "My hand hurts. I want to get some salve on it."

"Sure thing," the constable agreed. There was nothing more he and the deputy could do. They could come back in the morning, and search the area. "Are you sure you can walk?" they asked the shaken scoutmaster.

Smith took the deputy's arm and stumbled back to the road, the boys at his heels. In the glare of the car headlights, he checked his hand. It didn't look too bad. "It hurts worse than it looks. That could be a radioactive burn." The hair on his forearm was singed, and there was a burned hole in his hat. Other than that, he appeared to be all right. "I'm lucky to be alive," he blurted. "But say, it's late. These boys' folks will be worried. How about taking them home for me?"

Both cars left the scene. Each boy was returned safely to his home with an exciting story to tell. Parents called friends and relatives. Someone called the local newspaper. The reporter hurried to Smith's house. He talked at length with him and wrote up the story. It appeared in the morning newspaper, and by late afternoon was being reprinted in newspapers elsewhere.

When Captain Ruppelt of Project Blue Book heard the story a day or two later, he called the sheriff in West Palm Beach. Assured the account was correct, he and one of his staff flew to Florida to interview the scoutmaster.

Smith met with them. He showed them his hand, healed now save for a few singed hairs. He showed them the burned hole in his hat. When asked if he would permit them to send the hat north for analysis, he agreed. He gave them the machete, too. "You might want to check it for radiation," he said.

"Tell us something about your background," Captain Ruppelt asked, since this would give him a better idea of how reliable a person Mr. Smith was. The scoutmaster said he had gone to a military academy, had served in the Pacific during the war, and afterwards had run a gas station until he got his present job as a clerk in a hardware store. When a local church organized a Boy Scout troop, he had volunteered to be the scoutmaster.

"Now tell us exactly what happened," the Captain asked.

But Smith refused to say anything.

"Why not?" the surprised investigator asked.

Smith fumbled around and acted mysterious. "Someone warned me not to talk."

"Who?"

Finally Smith admitted that he had hired a press agent who was going to try to sell his story to a newspaper syndicate or a magazine.

After further attempts to get information had failed, Captain Ruppelt and his aide left Smith. But they went straight to the sheriff's office. The constable and deputy admitted there was something about Smith's story that "didn't hitch." They had gone over every foot of the area where they had found him. Not a twig was scorched. No tree tops were bent. No marks showed where an object might have landed. They had not noticed any peculiar odor. They had even gone back after dark and had maintained a watch for several hours. No UFO had appeared. Even if one had, they said they could not have seen it from the road because of the thick trees.

However, they had noticed one very significant detail. Planes approaching the county airport, and coming in with their landing lights on, could be seen swishing by in the darkness. Their lights flickered through the trees.

"We don't like to doubt the word of a scoutmaster, but his story isn't holding up well," the deputy said. "We checked the airport. Several planes did land during the time Smith was in the woods. We got in touch with the pilots. None saw anything out of the ordinary over that area."

The Project Blue Book men checked the area in daylight and after dark. They saw planes fly over with landing lights on. Then they questioned each boy separately. Each told the same story. Each also mentioned how Mr. Smith had brought up the subject of flying saucers while driving Johnny home.

"You're sure Mr. Smith brought this up?" the captain asked.

"Yes, sir," each insisted.

"Did you see a light flickering through the trees?"

Each had.

"Did you hear a plane?"

The boys honestly could not remember. They had been too excited about the possibility of there being a flying saucer in the woods.

"Did you see a dark round object with a dome hovering over the trees?"

Each most definitely had not.

"Did you smell anything peculiar when you found Mr. Smith?"

Again, no.

A new picture began to develop in the minds of the investigators, but they said nothing to the boys. They thanked them for their help and went away. But they questioned other townspeople about Smith. Slowly, hint by hint, a different story came out. Smith had not been in the war. He had been booted out of the Marines only a few months after his induction for being absent without leave and stealing a car. He had served time in a federal reformatory. He had been fired from the gas station job.

Since it was near midnight when the new picture of Smith was put together, Ruppelt and his assistant went to bed. The captain was wakened the next morning by a call from the Pentagon. A top official there informed him that, according to a front page story in a Washington newspaper, Smith was quoted as saying he had been questioned lengthily by "high brass from Washington."

Ruppelt sputtered. "Smith couldn't have said that. He knew we were from Dayton."

The Pentagon caller read further from the newspaper: "The scoutmaster said the Air Force knew what he [Smith] had seen, but he couldn't tell — it would create a national panic." the caller added, "We are swamped with calls from angry saucer fans. They want to know why 'high brass' have muzzled Smith." The caller then demanded that Ruppelt get the story straightened out — and fast!

Ruppelt groaned, said "Yes, sir" with the proper deference due a superior officer, and went to work. He placed calls to the Marine Corps and the federal reformatory. Both confirmed the facts about Smith. Since Smith refused to see them again, and there was nothing more to be learned in Florida, Ruppelt and his aide flew back to Dayton. ATIC experts said that the hat and machete showed no signs of radioactivity. The burn on the hat had very obviously been caused by a cigarette! The captain was not surprised. By now he was convinced Smith had singed the hairs on his hand by running a lighted match over them.

Captain Ruppelt gave his report to the newspapers. He said that in his opinion, the Smith story was a deliberate hoax. Apparently Smith had planned the whole deal with the hope of making some money by telling a fantastic story to a newspaper or a magazine.

Thanks to this publicity-seeking stunt, a lot of time and effort on the part of law officers and government investigators had been devoted, at the taxpayers' expense, to proving that Smith had perpetrated an out and out hoax.

The story about the scoutmaster has been included as an example of how a hoax can be planned and carried out. It is false reports which have damaged the serious approach to the problem of flying saucers and UFOs. Fortunately hoaxers are usually found out and discredited because of the careful work done by investigators.

7

Monsters from Outer Space

DURING THE FIRST five years of the flying-saucer craze, it was mostly strange lights, discs and windowed spacecraft which were reported. None had proved dangerous in any way, and none had landed. But in 1952 the first of two stories about menacing space creatures appeared in newspapers and magazines.

On the night of September 12, 1952, near Sutton, West Virginia, thousands of people saw a glowing object streak across the sky. Of these, a Mrs. May and her three sons and a seventeen-year-old National Guardsman named Gene Lemon were sure they saw something strange land on a hill near their home. Although it was dark, they climbed the slope to see it. One of the boys had a flashlight. As the five told it later, the first thing they noticed was a very disagreeable odor. Then two eyes shone in the beam of the flashlight. Then they all saw a huge figure, nine feet tall. It had a frightening, evil-looking face.

As the light stayed on it, the monster's body began to glow. The creature made a strange hissing sound and moved forward threateningly.

"Run!" Mrs. May screamed.

All fled to the May home, where Mrs. May called the sheriff. After hanging up the telephone, she noticed an oily film on her boys' faces. Their throats had begun to swell. She called a doctor, being positive the monster had sprayed the boys with some sort of gas.

The doctor arrived and examined the boys. Their throats were inflamed. He was puzzled. A person inhaling poisonous mustard gas would have had the same symptoms. Fortunately the boys recovered completely, but it took some time for them to get over their fright.

By the time the sheriff arrived, fog had settled over the hill. Nevertheless, he led his two bloodhounds toward the spot where the monster had been seen. The dogs ran away, howling. The sheriff left the scene but promised to come back the next day.

Soon after daylight a man telephoned the sheriff and said he had seen a strange machine rise from the hilltop. He said he had gone out to investigate and had found tracks on the ground, some trampled grass, and bits of black stuff like plastic. But there was no trace of the monster. The sheriff investigated but found nothing he considered was evidence that a strange visitor had been present. The black stuff looked like ordinary plastic.

The story appeared in newspapers all over the country and was broadcast over the radio. Later Mrs. May and the boys described their frighten-

ing experience on the program, "We, the People."
Neighbors, law officers, reporters and writers had
gone over the evidence in the meantime. Many
were convinced Mrs. May and the boys had
really seeing something and were not faking. The
Air Force did not investigate because it considered this a crackpot story. The excitement died
out, and nothing more was ever heard of the
Sutton monster.

Then in 1955 another story broke into print.
By coincidence, it also involved the name of
Sutton, a family this time, not a place. Because
the Sutton family of Kelly, Kentucky, had a good
reputation and obviously were badly frightened
by something, police officers were inclined to
believe they were telling the truth.

The story began about 7 P.M. on a Sunday
evening, August 2, on the Sutton farm near Kelly.
At that hour teenager Billy Sutton left the house
to fetch water from a well. Looking skyward, he
saw a glowing object slowly settle to the ground
behind the barn. He was not frightened but told
his family about it. The Suttons were entertain-
ing relatives at the time. All told, there were
eight adults and three children in the house.

They were not disturbed either. "You probably
saw a falling star," they told Billy.

Some time later the farm dogs began barking
excitedly.

"I better see what the ruckus is about," Elmer
Sutton said. "There might be a fox in the chicken
coop." He and John Sutton walked to the back
door and looked outside. There, as they later
told it, was a strange creature. "It glowed like the

numbers on a radium-painted watch," they told law officers during the subsequent investigation. Worse, the creature walked slowly toward them. It came close enough so they could see that it resembled a very small man, not even four feet tall, with a very large head, very long arms and hands that were webbed and ended in claws. The creature wore a shiny suit.

Mrs. Sutton came to the door and also saw the creature. She remembered later, "It was as shiny as aluminum foil, and it walked like a very old man — or some sort of monkey — mostly with its hands."

The two men rushed for guns. Elmer fired a twelve-gauge shotgun at the creature, and John a .22-caliber pistol. They heard at least one shot ricochet, as if bouncing off something metallic. The creature fell backwards when shot but immediately popped up and ran away.

That alarmed the two men so much that they ran back into the house shouting, "Turn out the lights! Lock the doors!" The women and children threw themselves on the floor. The children started to cry, but their mothers made them be still.

After a bit someone turned on a light. One of the women screamed, "Look!"

A helmeted creature with wide slit eyes was peering in the dining room window.

Elmer and John fired at it. Window glass and screen shattered; the creature fell back. After this everyone in the house remained absolutely silent, waiting tensely for the creature to appear again.

About twenty minutes later, when nothing had

happened, Elmer, John, and Billy crept out into the yard. Off to the side something glowed in a tree. The dogs were in a frenzy, leaping and barking at it. The men started toward the tree when Billy gasped, "There's another one!"

Up on the roof of the house was another creature. Elmer fired his shotgun at it. He and the others heard the shot strike something and saw the creature dive to the ground and run off through a weed patch.

The Suttons turned back toward the tree where they had seen the glowing object. They shot at it. The dogs fled under the house, and the glowing object *floated* to the ground and vanished.

Once more the Sutton men returned to the house. Everyone sat in the dark for two hours. The suspense was almost unbearable. The men stood guard by the windows, but no more creatures appeared.

Finally the family decided to report the incident to the police. Since they had no phone, they piled into two cars and sped to the nearest station, eight miles away at Hopkinsville, Kentucky. When they burst in on Police Chief Russell Greenwell, everybody talked at once. It was some time before the chief got a clear, step-by-step story. The fact that the Suttons were so frightened made him feel that the tale was true. He alerted four policemen and returned with them to the Sutton farm. He also notified the State Police. On their way to the farm, the State Troopers saw several "meteors" coming from the direction of the Sutton place. These swished low over their cars and disappeared. When the troopers arrived, they joined the police in searching the house and grounds.

The lawmen found nothing. The ground was so hard and dry that no footprints could have been left. There were no marks to indicate where a spacecraft might have rested. But there were bullet holes and shattered window glass to show that the Suttons had indeed shot at something.

The next day Police Chief Greenwell let the local newspaper in on the story. He and his men talked to Sutton neighbors. All agreed they were a fine family, not given to drinking or wild doings.

Reporters descended on the farm and questioned everyone, but the published story caused little excitement elsewhere. By this time most Americans were used to stories about people who saw strange creatures. And the fantastic tale was soon forgotten.

8

Little Men

IT IS A STRIKING FACT that reports of so-called creatures from outer space can be divided into two types. One speaks of great, horrible monsters, but another describes space dwellers as harmless little beings who are indifferent to or actually shy of the inhabitants of earth.

People call them "little men" or "little green men" or "humanoids," but mean the same thing. These little creatures pop up in science-fiction tales, and usually are described as being small and wearing suits somewhat like those our astronauts wear in their space travels. In every state there are people who claim they have seen these creatures and have even carried on conversations with them. No one really pays much attention to these stories. But occasionally reliable people do report some amazing experiences involving "little men." Here are a few examples of such reports. One originated in New Guinea, one in Canada, one in Tasmania, and one right here in the United States.

On the evening of June 26, 1957, the Reverend William B. Gill stepped out on the porch of the Anglican Mission located at Boainai, in remote New Guinea. Reverend Gill was an ordained minister in the Church of England. For thirteen years he had been active in church mission work. Up to the very moment of his experience, he had thought flying saucers were, as he said, "strictly a figment of imagination, or some electrical phenomenon."

Briefly, here is Reverend Gill's story, drawn from his written account and countersigned by those with him at the time.

After dinner Reverend Gill strolled out onto the porch of the mission house. He looked skyward and saw the planet Venus. But then he saw another bright, sparkling object. As it approached, Gill called to those still in the dining room, "Come out here. Hurry!"

A teacher and several students rushed to his side. All watched an object approach within four hundred feet of them. They could see it was a huge disc-shaped craft, possibly thirty to forty feet wide. Four metal legs, or antennae, protruded from the underside. On top was a dome some ten feet high, and above this a deck. Four creatures were clearly visible on the deck. They seemed to be working on a thin blue spotlight that blinked off and on.

Gill wrote, "As one of them leaned over the rail or whatever it was and seemed to be looking down on us, I waved one hand overhead, and the figure did the same, like a skipper on a boat waving to someone on the wharf. The teacher beside me waved both arms over his head, and two figures on the craft did the same. Then both of us waved both arms aloft, and all four of the figures did the same in response. We were all delighted. The boys were jubilant. Some of them called out to the figures on the disc, but we heard no response. One of the boys brought out a flashlight, and we turned the beam on the object. It hovered — and came quite close to the ground. We thought it was going to land, but it did not. We were very disappointed about that."

The Gill statement does not say how, or how much later, the disc disappeared. But it did reappear several times during the same week and was observed by a total of thirty-seven people. But it never came close enough so Gill and his friends could see the creatures' faces.

Australian newspapers gave a great deal of space to this story. Their reporters visited the site and investigated the minister's reputation. He was much respected, popular, intelligent, and not given to telling wild tales. His report was concise, and as exact in detail as he could make it. None of the observers had been panicky or frightened. On the contrary, they had been curious and clearheaded enough to make signs encouraging the space visitors to land. The written report filled eleven, single-spaced typewritten pages. It is the only report of its kind and hard to disprove. Believable or not, it makes good reading.

The next story comes from Canada.

An executive of the Steep Rock Mines in Ontario and his wife were boating on Steep Rock Lake on July 2, 1950. They turned into a deep hidden cove, reaching it through a narrow gateway formed by huge boulders. The couple had visited the cove before. They pulled the boat up on the narrow beach shadowed by overhanging tree limbs and had a picnic lunch. It was a beautiful place to relax.

Not long afterward, they felt the air vibrate strongly, as it would have after a big explosion.

"What was that?" the wife said.

Her husband answered, "Oh, probably a shock wave from a dynamite blast at the mine."

"But there was no sound, and we're miles from the mine."

"You're right." The man thought a moment. He looked at the boulder behind him. "I'm going to climb up that rock. I ought to be able to look out over the lake from there, and see if anything is wrong."

"Do be careful," his wife warned.

With some effort the man climbed to the top of the boulder. He found the top was split, and he could look out through a sharp cleft. The first thing he saw was a large shiny object floating on the water just beyond the narrow entrance to the cove. The sight was so fantastic that he scrambled down to get his wife. Both returned to the well-hidden viewpoint.

"It was still there," the man said later in telling his story. "It looked like two huge saucers stuck together. It was some forty-five feet wide, about fifteen feet thick at the center, and possibly twelve feet thick at the rim. There were round black-edged ports, or windows, about four feet apart around the rim. Hatch covers on the topside were open. Moving slowly around over its surface were about ten queer-looking creatures. Over their heads was a hoop-shaped object rotating slowly from a central position."

When the hoop reached a point directly opposite the couple, it stopped. So did the figures. They remained motionless, staring toward the couple's hiding place.

The wife tugged at her husband's sleeve. "Duck!"

Both did. They were sure the creatures had spotted them. They remained hidden until the husband noticed that a deer below had come to the water to drink. Hoping the strange men were watching the deer, the man and woman rose for another look.

They saw that the hoop was rotating once more. It was operated by a creature standing beneath it. The operator wore a bright red skull cap and was about four feet tall. The others were the same size, but wore blue helmets and close-fitting dark suits. The most frightening thing was that the figures appeared to be robots, though the report did not say in what way. The couple was too far away to see whether the creatures had human facial features.

One of the figures put a bright green hose in the water. He appeared to draw water through it and at the same time discharged something from another hose.

Once more the hoop stopped rotating, and all the figures froze. They stared toward the couple on the rock. The man and wife ducked and counted to twenty. When they inched up for another look, the creatures were out of sight, the hatches were closed, and the disc was slowly rising from the water. It streaked out of sight, leaving a patch of reddish-blue water where it had floated.

The couple climbed down to their boat. After waiting awhile, they decided the spaceship was not going to return and went home. When they told friends what had happened, one man said, "There must have been something awfully strong in that tea you drank!"

Other friends did believe them, however, and made a trip to the cove. The strange craft reappeared. However, when this second group of observers tried to approach it, the little figures popped down the hatches, and the disc soared out of sight in a great rush of wind.

The couple who had first seen the saucer refused to tell their story to a newspaper. Much later, however, they did allow the editor of the mining company magazine to print an account of it providing he did not use their names. A flying-saucer fan happened to see a copy, and sent it to Frank Edwards, who included it in his book *Flying Saucers: Serious Business*.

The next tale comes from far-away Hobart, Tasmania.

A high-school teacher named Mrs. E. D. Sylvester was driving on a road near there about 7:30 P.M. on the evening of October 28, 1962. She had with her her three children, aged ten, eight, and six years old. All four saw an object swoop across the road far out in front of them.

"What was that, Mum?" the children asked excitedly.

"It looked like a flying saucer!" the ten-year-old exclaimed.

"Nonsense," their very sensible mother answered. She had taught school long enough to know how easily excitable children's imaginations can be.

Before long their car reached the place where the strange object had crossed the road.

"Mum, let's have a look!"

Mrs. Sylvester stopped the car. All four walked some distance off the road and came upon an egg-shaped craft. Mrs. Sylvester said quietly, "Stay back." She studied the strange craft and judged it was about fifteen feet long and maybe five or six feet wide. It rested on the ground.

The older boy tugged at her sleeve. "Mum, look over there!"

Beyond the craft was a little man. He wore a close-fitting, silver-colored suit. A translucent helmet covered his head and appeared to be connected by a tube to some contraption on his back. He had a shiny box in his hands and was putting samples of earth into it.

Mrs. Sylvester motioned the children to remain absolutely quiet. They did so. Since their mother was not frightened, they calmed down. For forty minutes they watched the small creature dart about, picking up samples of soil. He appeared not to notice them, and in time reentered the craft and buzzed away.

Mrs. Sylvester reported the sighting to government authorities. There was brief mention in a local newspaper, and then the story was forgotten. If a copy of the story had not eventually reached the hands of a flying-saucer fan in the United States, it might have remained unknown. It has since been widely reprinted in magazines and flying-saucer books and is a favorite among those who believe space creatures are visiting earth.

About the time everyone becomes convinced that all stories of "little men" are hoaxes, something really puzzling is reported. The following incident happened at Socorro, New Mexico, in 1964. The Air Force sent both ATIC investigators and a well-known scientist to work on it, and NICAP also sent a man to the scene.

On the afternoon of April 24, a long-time police officer named Lonnie Zamora was driving about Socorro in a patrol car. Suddenly he saw something shiny descend into a gully just outside the small town. Moments later he heard a loud roaring sound. Knowing there was an old dynamite shed in the area, Patrolman Zamora immediately reported the incident to headquarters on his car radio and took off to find out what had happened. He turned off the main road out of town and followed a winding road to the top of a hill. From there he looked along a gully and about a half mile away saw what appeared to be at first glance an overturned automobile. It was white and turned on end. Alongside it were two figures in white coveralls, about four feet high.

Zamora radioed in what he had discovered and said he was going to investigate. By following the road, he was able to come within a hundred yards of the object. The figures in white coveralls were no longer in sight, but a white egg-shaped craft, sitting on four legs and about the size of a car, was very much in evidence. Zamora approached it until a sudden roar from it made him race for some sheltering bushes. The craft rose twenty feet off the ground, hovered silently long enough for him to notice a design in red letters on the side. Later Zamora described this as "a crescent with a vertical arrow pointed upward and a horizontal bar beneath it." Seconds later the strange craft flew out of sight.

The police officer scrambled back to his car and radioed in what he had seen. Very shortly another police car raced up. Sergeant Chavez piled out of his cruiser and asked, "What's going on here?"

Although still excited, Zamora told a straight story. Then he and Chavez went down into the gully. They found four deep round marks where the metallic legs might have rested on the ground. One rock had a sort of metallic scratch on it. The bushes and ground were smoking, as if seared by a jet flame. But the hard-packed sand underfoot revealed no footprints.

Returning to their cars, both officers reported what they had observed. The news of this astonishing sighting was sped on to a military base in the area. Immediately intelligence officers were ordered to the scene. They saw the holes in the ground, and the singed bushes. After going over the area very carefully, they placed rocks around the hole marks. The next morning they returned with a camera and photographed them.

Since the initial report had come from two police officers of fine reputation, the intelligence officers alerted Project Blue Book, which sent an officer to the scene. Another arrived from Kirtland Air Force Base at Albuquerque. Then the Air Force asked its civilian expert on aerial phenomena, Dr. J. Allen Hynek, to make an on-the-spot review.

Patrolmen Zamora and Chavez underwent days of questioning. The Project Blue Book officer wondered if the craft could have been a secret "super pogo" device being built by the military. He checked and found it was not. He also learned the craft could not have been a meteor, or a balloon, or any of the usual objects mistaken for a UFO.

Meantime a NICAP member arrived and conducted a separate investigation. He gathered soil samples and a fragment of the shiny material scraped on the rock and sent them and his data to NICAP headquarters. The samples were turned over to a government laboratory for analysis, because NICAP does not have the facilities to do this and must rely on other agencies for such analyses. Nothing startling or conclusive was learned from the Socorro samples or data.

Seldom has a sighting received a more thorough investigation. But as late as January 1966 the official Air Force conclusion was, "The case has been well investigated and analyzed by experts. But it is still a mystery." NICAP accepts this conclusion.

One thing is certain: This will not be the last report we will hear about "little men."

9

Unexplained Pilot Sightings

PILOTS ARE AMONG the best-qualified people to have made UFO sightings. Their long, exacting training, their study of aerial phenomena, and especially their familiarity with night skies give them a superb background. Thus a pilot should know, if anyone does, how to observe and report the sighting of an unidentified flying object.

From 1948 to 1959, some truly astonishing sightings were made by both commercial and military pilots. Unfortunately in the publicity accompanying some of these cases, the pilots were so ridiculed and contradicted that gradually most pilots began to refuse to make public any details of unusual sightings. As required by law, they do report UFOs to airport traffic control crews, but the story goes no further. Many airline companies frown on publicity about their pilots' sightings. They cannot be blamed for this because they are naturally anxious that the public have the greatest confidence in their pilots and not worry about UFOs approaching airliners. The Air Force regulations forbid its pilots and personnel to make public information on sightings, even when they are made by pilots who have been sent aloft to intercept a reported UFO and get a radar beam on the object. However, on occasion the Air Force declassifies information on a few old sightings, so the public eventually hears about them. The details of a few are given here.

On the night of July 24, 1948, an Eastern Airlines DC-3 passenger liner took off from Houston, Texas, on a routine flight to Boston. It was a bright moonlit night. The pilot was Captain Clarence S. Chiles. During World War II Chiles had been a lieutenant colonel in the Air Transport Command. He had 8,500 flying hours to his credit. The First Officer was John B. Whitted, also an experienced airman. The flight was uneventful until 2:45 A.M., when the DC-3 was nearing Montgomery, Alabama.

Suddenly the pilot saw a very bright light dead ahead. It approached so swiftly that he immediately ruled out the possibility of its being another plane. He tapped Whitted on the arm and pointed to it. In those few seconds the light zoomed so close that Chiles was positive there would be a collision. He racked the DC-3 into a tight left turn. The light flashed by not more than 700 feet from the big airship. Chiles instantly leveled off and resumed his regular flight pattern.

"Did you get a good look at it?" he asked. Although he had remained calm during the emergency, his heart was hammering.

Whitted nodded. "I thought I saw a double-decked spaceship!"

Chiles agreed. He contacted the control tower at the Montgomery airport. After identifying his flight number, he asked, "Are there any other aircraft in the area?"

He learned there were not. Then he gave his report. He said the strange craft was cigar-shaped, about 100 feet long, and twice the diameter of a B-29. It had no wings, and something like a radar pole protruded from the nose. It was double-decked, with two rows of lighted windows on its side. The light coming from them was bluish-white and phosphorescent. Neither he nor Whitted could see anyone inside the ship.

"Just as it went by," Chiles related, "it pulled up sharp — as if whoever was piloting it had seen us and wanted to avoid hitting us. The craft then zoomed into the clouds. A fifty-foot trail of orange-red flame shot from its rear. Its jet wash rocked our DC-3."

The air control operator exclaimed, "Repeat. Did you say a double-decked spaceship?"

"A double-decked spaceship."

With his report finished, Captain Chiles flew on to Boston. After landing, he made a written report for the airline company and another for the Civilian Aviation Agency, which was the federal agency then charged with air traffic and control. He also talked to newspaper reporters.

As could be expected, the story was a sensation. The Air Force sent ATIC investigators to question him and his copilot. Since one of the passengers had reported seeing "a strange eerie streak of light," they questioned him also. Several days later an Air Force spokesman at the

Pentagon said that what Chiles and Whitted had seen was really a shooting star.

The pilot and copilot were angry at having their word doubted. They felt the statement cast doubt on their ability as pilots and their reliability as honest observers. They were positive they had *not* seen a shooting star because they had seen many shooting stars before, and the UFO had not been anything like them. However, the pilots were not able to bring about a change in the Pentagon statement because they could not offer concrete proof that what they had seen was really a double-decked spaceship.

By January of 1952 the file of UFO sightings reported to Project Blue Book filled several drawers. Captain Ruppelt, who was in charge then, asserted that seventy-five per cent were cases of sincere observers mistaking meteors, stars, and balloons for unidentified flying objects. About five per cent were outright hoaxes. That left twenty per cent assigned to the file marked *Unexplained*.

One of the latter was the experience of a Trans World Airlines pilot flying a C-54 cargo airplane between Chicago and Kansas City. On the afternoon of March 8, 1952, this plane was flying 500 feet above a solid overcast, when both pilot and copilot saw a silver disc some distance off their left wing.

"Balloon," the pilot said.

"Looks like it," the copilot answered.

The two watched it off and on for five minutes. It remained in the same position. A balloon could not have done that; it would have dropped back.

The pilot did some checking. He turned left gradually toward the disc. It veered left and kept the same distance.

"That darn thing should have dropped behind us! We made a 45-degree turn."

"Try a right turn."

The pilot did, and the UFO followed. He completed a full circle. Although the UFO remained out to the side of the C-54, it completed the circle too.

The pilot remarked, "Well, that shot our balloon idea in the head. Let's give 'er full power." The copilot did, on all four engines. The C-54 climbed several thousand feet, and then the pilot started a long glide toward the UFO. It dropped down and disappeared into the overcast. But seconds later it streaked past the plane's right wing and disappeared into the sky.

The pilot radioed the nearest airport control tower, and learned there were neither planes nor balloons in the vicinity. Later, when Captain Ruppelt questioned him, the pilot vowed he had seen an interplanetary spacecraft. He kept saying, "I tell you, somebody had to be directing that thing!"

While not doubting his word, Captain Ruppelt filed the information in the file of folders marked *Unexplained*. No official statement was ever issued on it.

Another sighting early in July of 1952 caused a great stir in military channels but was not made public until some of the details appeared in Captain Ruppelt's book. It was kept quiet because the pilot was a member of the Air Force, and the Air

Force has strict rules about making public any sighting made by its people until years have passed. Although the captain was allowed to include the story in his book, he was not allowed to give the exact date, or location, or name of the pilot. Here are some of the details he did include.

One morning the radarscope at a fighter base showed an unidentified blip coming in very fast, about 700 miles an hour. Radar technicians are trained so they can chart the movement of a blip on the scope and estimate the approximate speed and distance covered by an aircraft. Soon this particular UFO slowed to a speed of 100 miles an hour. Two F-86 interceptor jets were scrambled; that is, they were ordered out to intercept it.

A little later, when the jets were airborne, the unidentified blip began to fade off the radarscope. Thinking that the craft represented by the blip had flown either too high or too low to show on the scope, the operator radioed both pilots to climb to 40,000 feet and look around. They did and saw nothing. He ordered one down to 20,-000 feet and the other down to 5,000 feet. Both pilots made quick descents.

The pilot at 5,000 feet noticed a bright flash below and ahead of him. He reported this on the radio and made a beeline for it. As he closed in, he was sure he was looking at a weather balloon. Moments later he realized this could not be so because no balloon could keep out in front of him at the speed he was flying. So he poured on the power and came closer, within 1,000 yards. Now the object appeared to be saucer-shaped. He tried to report this to the tower but could not make contact on his radio. He tried to call the F-86 flying above him but could not get through. This used up two minutes. In that time he came within 500 feet of the UFO.

Suddenly it began to pull away. The pilot realized he would never catch it. The distance between them lengthened to 1,000 yards again. Seeing he was about to lose his quarry, the pilot made a quick decision. He trained his gun on the UFO and cut loose with a round of fire. The UFO streaked out of sight. The pilot turned back and landed. He reported the incident to his squadron commander, who called in his superior officers to question the pilot. They were angry because an Air Force pilot is never to fire on a craft unless it makes hostile moves.

The squadron commander accused the pilot of either cracking up or firing his gun for the fun of it and then making up a wild story to cover up.

The pilot vigorously denied this. He stuck to his story about the UFO. The radar man backed him up. Other pilots and the flight surgeon were brought in to testify as to the pilot's mental condition. All said he was a very sound person and a fine pilot. So, after receiving a scorching lecture for firing on a craft that had made no hostile moves, the pilot was dismissed without further reprimand. The details of this incident were in the file of unsolved sightings.

Another unexplained pilot sighting occurred shortly before daylight on December 6, 1952, when a B-29 bomber was flying over the Gulf of Mexico. The crew had been on a routine practice run between Florida and Texas. The night was clear, the stars brilliant.

At 5:24 A.M. Captain John Harter got on the intercom and called the radar officer, Lieutenant Sidney Coleman. "Turn on the radar. I want to check the coastline." The captain estimated they were about 100 miles south of Louisiana but wanted to be sure. He would check the nearness of the coastline by viewing an auxiliary radarscope located in his cockpit.

Lieutenant Coleman turned on the set. Lights glowed, and the sweep hand began circling the screen. A blip appeared on the edge. Coleman noted its location and the time. He watched it as the sweep hand completed another revolution.

"Holy smoke!" In those few seconds the blip had moved a distance which he figured was about fifteen miles. Still watching, he groped for a stop watch and started it so he could have a more exact measurement of time. He said to the flight engineer sitting next to him, "Bailey, I've got an unidentified blip moving at a fantastic speed on this scope. Help me track it."

The two men watched tensely. The blip loomed brighter and a little closer. "It's on a collision course with us!" Coleman hollered.

The engineer's pencil flew over a paper pad. "It figures out 5,240 miles per hour!"

Coleman dropped the watch and grabbed the intercom mike. "Captain, Bailey and I just tracked an unknown at over 5,000 miles per hour. Check your set."

Captain Harter said, "Impossible. Check *your* set."

Coleman did this. Bailey watched the screen. "There's another one!"

At that moment the navigator, Lieutenant Cassidy, announced over the intercom, "I've got two unidentified blips on my scope."

Coleman worked fast, straining hard for accuracy. Before he had finished, Bailey shouted, "Now there are four of 'em!"

The pilot called, "I have four unknowns at twelve o'clock. What do you show?"

"Twelve o'clock" meant a position dead ahead. Coleman said, "They're on all scopes, sir. Recalibration [rechecking] shows no error."

Captain Harter watched the blips move across his auxiliary set more swiftly than any he had ever seen, and he had viewed thousands of normal blips. When one veered, he shouted, "Unknown at three o'clock!"

In the compartment behind the cockpit, the flight engineer leaped to the right waist blister. Nose against the glass, he peered out. An unidentified object glowing with blue-white light whipped by in a blur. It vanished below the bomber. Before he could turn around, Coleman shouted, "They're gone!" The screen was completely empty.

Shaking a little, Bailey returned to his seat. He reported what he had seen to the pilot. Harter had seen the same thing. Coleman said, "I could watch the track of the one that went by us, but the other three just winked out."

For a few moments the situation was normal. The bomber droned on its steady course. But less than three minutes later Coleman yelled, "They're back!"

The pilot and navigator also saw the blips on their sets. All approached at incredible speed, then veered a hairbreadth to the right. Captain Harter called, "Unknown at three o'clock!" And once more a lighted object streaked by. Then the radar screens were empty again.

One minute went by. Two. Three.

Coleman relaxed a little. "Maybe we're rid of 'em. What do you think they were?"

Bailey joked, "Flying saucers."

"Quit kidding. I'm serious. Do you think we've got secret weapons that will go that fast?"

The flight engineer shook his head. "Impossible. There's a lot of scuttlebutt floating around about some experimental jet flying at supersonic speed, but nothing like 5,000 miles an hour."

"It had to be a meteor."

"But there were four blips. A meteor would only show as one. And the blasted things came back. A meteor would never do that."

"Well, maybe it was breaking up."

In all his training, the flight engineer had never heard of a meteor breaking up into identical-sized fragments that kept pace with each other on a straight course. Invariably meteors traveled in a broad arc, with an earthward trend. "Hang it, I've heard plenty of talk about UFO's and always laughed them off. Now I'm wondering if I imagined what I saw."

"Well, if you did, so did the rest of us," the radar officer said.

One of the crew, a staff sergeant named Ferris, joined them. "A little excitement, hunh?"

"Plenty."

"Can I watch?"

Coleman nodded. "You probably won't see anything." Nevertheless, Ferris stood quietly behind him.

Six minutes later Coleman yelled, "They're back again!" He grabbed the stop watch and began calling off times and distance to the engineer.

Bailey figured hurriedly. "Same speed as before."

The pilot's voice was heard. "Unknowns at four o'clock."

This time it was Ferris who dashed toward the waist blister and saw two blurs of blue-white light streak by.

In the cockpit Captain Harter saw the same thing. He also saw the track of the unidentified craft as they passed on the right and raced out of radar range. Seconds later, five reappeared. They were behind the bomber but cutting across its course. Then Harter froze as he watched them swerve and head right for the B-29.

Even before he could move toward the controls to take evasive action, the blips' forward motion stopped cold. Sweat broke out on Harter's forehead and ran down his face. He held his breath. The blips began to move again, but at the same speed as his ship. They were trailing the bomber!

Ten seconds clicked by. The blips moved off to one side. Then a huge blip twice the size of the others flared brilliantly on his auxiliary scope. Whatever it was, radar was receiving a very solid return. The four smaller blips veered toward the large one and *merged with it*. The larger blip flared again with almost blinding brilliance and then flashed across the scope and off the set.

The intercom speaker clicked. The pilot heard Coleman stammer, "C-c-captain, did you see what I saw?"

"Yes, I saw it."

The navigator said he had seen it also.

Coleman added, "Bailey figured that big blip was going 9,000 miles an hour when it passed out of our radar range."

"Keep watch," the pilot said, although the order was superfluous. Navigator, flight engineer and radar officer were all but glued to the scopes for the rest of the flight. The pilot radioed ahead, and gave his report of the weird sightings. By the time the B-29 landed at its home base in Texas, intelligence officers from a nearby air base were waiting to question the crew.

First, Captain Harter gave his story. He told of the first and second sightings. Of the third group, he said, "One group of blips was noted, after the set was checked for accuracy, to arc about and swing in behind us and maintain speed and distance for approximately ten seconds. Contact was broken off at 0535, after a group of the blips merged into a one-half-inch arc and proceeded across the scope and off it at a computed speed of over 9,000 miles per hour."

The intelligence officers gasped. "Are you trying to tell us that these UFOs were sighted three times and then merged with some sort of mother ship that whisked them out of range?"

The pilot answered, "The assumption about a mother ship is yours, sir."

The investigators questioned the others. "You're sure you checked that set correctly?"

Coleman said he had double-checked it in between sightings, and afterward, and it was working perfectly.

Next the intelligence officers questioned each crewman separately. They did everything they could to punch holes in the story. They kept exclaiming, "But what you are saying is that there was a mother ship hovering about, that these discs were sent out to track the B-29, and after they did this, they were taken on board again and flown out of radar range."

Each of the crew said politely, "I didn't say anything about a mother ship. You did, sir. I didn't describe the objects as discs. You did, sir. I said they were streaks of bluish-white light." Finally the tired crew was dismissed. The intelligence officers checked with the weather service. There were no exceptionally bright stars, no comets or meteors, no temperature inversions in the area at the time of the sighting. There were no balloons aloft and no other aircraft within radar range.

The data was sent on to Project Blue Book. Captain Ruppelt flew to Texas and questioned the crew. Not one of them changed his story. The captain even ran a check on each airman's physical and mental condition. All were in excellent health and had no mental quirks.

Realizing there was nothing more to be learned, Project Blue Book closed the investigation. The "case of the mother ship" is still marked *Unexplained*. No publicity was given the sighting until after the data had been declassified and Captain Ruppelt had included them in his book.

You may have noticed that all these incidents happened several years ago. Today there is almost no information given out on sightings made by commercial airline pilots, and none by military pilots. Occasionally a private pilot speaks out about what he has seen, but there is usually so much ridicule that he clams up. One point must be stressed here. Hundreds of pilots fly over our country day and night without ever seeing a UFO. But when they do sight one, they should be able to make public their information without being ridiculed or harassed, because they are among our most skilled observers.

10

Some Famous
Photographs of UFOs

SOME OF THE MOST interesting evidence which flying-saucer enthusiasts present to prove that "something is up there" are the photographs which observers have been able to take of UFOs. Here are the stories of five people who were fortunate enough to obtain good pictures.

For several days during the first week of August in 1965, sky watchers from North Dakota to Mexico had been flooding radio and police stations with reports of bright-colored lights streaking back and forth across the heavens. There were single lights that hovered and zipped up and down. There were multiple lights, some flying in triangle formations and making sharp right-angle turns. Some were seen very high in the sky, others at almost ground level. In a few cases, the glowing UFOs actually remained motionless for a short period.

Because the newspapers headlined the sightings, a great many people stepped outside this clear night of August 3 to watch for them. Among these was A. L. Smith, a turbine engine consultant for American Airlines. He had also imparted his enthusiasm for planes to his fourteen-year-old son Alan. On this warm evening, father and son and three neighbors sat out in the Smith yard. Night sky watching can be fun even under normal circumstances. There is always the chance one will see a falling star of a glowing satellite gliding swiftly overhead. The men smoked, while Alan held onto a camera. It was an inexpensive model with a small view finder. His father told him his chance of snapping a picture of a UFO with any camera, let alone one of this kind, was exceedingly small. Alan didn't care. He kept it ready, just in case.

At midnight Mr. Smith suggested Alan go to bed. Alan did some tall talking and wangled permission to stay up a little longer. About 1:30 A.M. a multicolored lighted object appeared in the sky. They all watched with increasing amazement as it glided toward them. Suddenly, it appeared to hover several hundred yards away. Alan quickly raised his camera. He could not see the light in the view finder, but he aimed the camera at the object anyway and snapped the shutter. Since he could not see in the darkness to turn the film forward to the next number, he ran into the house to do this. Unfortunately by the time he rejoined his father, the UFO had vanished.

Alan brought the film in for processing. He could hardly wait to get it back. When he did, he was in for a big disappointment. There was no print of a UFO, only the negative.

Mr. Smith explained, "The photofinisher didn't

develop this negative because it's all dark. Nothing shows on it."

"But I aimed right at the light," Alan insisted. He took the shade off a lamp, and held the negative close to the lighted bulb. "Dad, look! There is something here in the lower righthand corner. It's a spot of light! I bet that's the UFO!"

Mr. Smith thought so too. Anyway, the negative was worth enlarging. He took it to a processor who magnified the lower righthand corner many times and made a print of it.

When he saw the print, Alan whooped. There was the UFO on film! It was shaped like a disc and was divided into three parts, with cloudy bands between them. The sections were blue-green, orange-yellow, and white.

"Yippeeee!" Alan shouted.

Mr. Smith called the editor of the Oklahoma City *Journal,* who was very interested and got the full story from Alan. Then the film was checked by experts to prove it had not been faked. Assured it was genuine, the editor ran the picture of the UFO and Alan and his story on page one of the newspaper.

Alan found himself the center of a lot of excitement and attention. The photograph was a sensation. It was reprinted later in other newspapers. When it appeared in the Indianapolis *Tribune,* over one hundred thousand copies were sold.

Of course, a copy of the photograph and the story were sent on to Project Blue Book. The Air Force did not say whether or not it believed Alan's picture was genuine but did say that the print was not of a UFO but of the phenomenon known as "electrical plasma." In contrast, the man who investigated the incident for NICAP stated that he thought the photograph was genuine and did depict a UFO.

So far the mystery of this sighting has never been solved. Alan's photograph is still reprinted frequently as one of the few of a UFO.

An even better daytime photograph of strange craft was also taken on August 3 by a man named Rex Heflin near Santa Ana, California. Mr. Heflin was employed as a Highway Accident Investigator for the Los Angeles County Highway Commission. Part of his work was to photograph accidents, so he always carried a Polaroid camera for this purpose. The camera was equipped with an electric eye that automatically controlled the proper exposure setting.

According to Mr. Heflin, he was driving near Santa Ana when he saw an unusual object coming toward him through the air. He stopped the truck, grabbed his camera, and snapped the shutter, while still sitting inside the truck. Then he counted off the required number of seconds while the picture was developing inside the camera. During this interval he switched on his two-way radio and tried to contact his office. The radio, which had worked perfectly only moments earlier, was now out of order. By this time he could pull the print of the picture from the camera. A quick glance told him he had a good shot. Quickly, while the strange object continued to zip about, he snapped a second, and then a third picture. In between shots, he had no luck with the radio. As the UFO moved off, he stepped out of the truck and took one last picture before the object vanished. Then he tried the radio once more and found it working again. He reported the sighting to his office and said he would be in shortly with the startling films.

What Mr. Heflin got were sharp, clear photographs of a strange object that looked somewhat like a metallic straw hat, flying at an angle. In two shots, the rear view mirror of his truck could be seen. On the third, the foreground was included. On the side of the road directly under the UFO was a round patch of swirling sand and debris. The surrounding ground was not disturbed.

Somehow the United Press International News Bureau heard about the pictures. It asked permission to study them, and Mr. Heflin gladly granted it. After examining them, one of the UPI photographers used a similar Polaroid at the same place and hour and was satisfied that the Heflin photos were not faked. The story was given considerable publicity. When the clippings and copies of the films were sent on to Project Blue Book, Major Quintanella labeled them a photographic hoax.

Several civilian and professional photographers came to Mr. Heflin's defense. They studied the prints thoroughly and pronounced them genuine. A member of NICAP interviewed Mr. Heflin, and sent his data and copies of the prints back to NICAP headquarters. NICAP also decided the photographs were genuine. Now widely reprinted in books and magazines, the Heflin photographs provide some of the best detailed daytime pictures of an unidentified flying object.

Scarcely a week after Alan Smith and Rex Heflin had shot their pictures, another teenager came up with a startling nighttime photograph. He was seventeen-year-old James Lucci of Beaver, Pennsylvania, a town north of Pittsburgh.

James knew cameras because his father was a photographer for the Air National Guard and had taught James and his brother a good deal about photographic procedure. James's hobby was photographing the moon and stars, a project that takes considerable care and skill.

On the evening of August 8, James was taking time exposures of the moon. His camera, a Yashika 635 precision model, was set up on a tripod in the family driveway. His father, his brother and a friend were watching him. At about 11:30 P.M. a large round object bigger than the moon appeared from behind a high hill in back of the house. James exposed the film for six seconds, released the shutter, and wound down for a second shot. He took that one and tried for a third, but by that time the UFO had disappeared.

The next day when the films were developed, James yelled, "Wow!" What he had was a picture of a brightly lighted disc with a whirling halo of light underneath it, rather like the tail of a kite.

The rest of the Lucci family were as excited as James. However, after talking things over, they decided not to say too much about the photograph. They did not want to get involved in the ridicule and unfavorable publicity that hounded flying-saucer observers. But they did tell close friends, and these people insisted James show his pictures to the editor of the *Beaver County Times*. The newspaper's photographer made some complicated tests and proved to his satisfaction that the pictures were genuine. The editor checked on the boy's reputation and found that the chief of police and high-school principal spoke very highly of him. So the editor decided to publish the best of James's three films.

The Air Force made no comment about this photograph either. Later, a physicist guessed that Lucci had actually photographed electrical plasma, or ball lightning, generated by high-tension wires crossing the neighborhood. But you can't convince the Lucci family that James didn't get a picture of a genuine UFO. NICAP supports this belief and points out how markedly similar James's UFO is to the one in Alan Smith's picture.

Still another series of photographs of a UFO was taken in the daytime by Dan and Grant Jaroslaw from the back yard of their home fifteen miles northeast of Detroit, Michigan, during the week of January 9, 1967. Unfortunately the exact date was not given in the nationwide coverage of the story by the Associated Press and based on a copyrighted story printed by the Detroit *News*. The press release said in part:

An Air Force consultant and leading authority on so-called flying saucers said Monday [January 16, 1967] that pictures of a hamburger-shaped object, snapped by two Michigan teen-agers, appear authentic and tend to support reports of similar sightings.

"The striking thing to me is the similarity these pictures have to other photos I have seen and also to verbal descriptions I've taken from ostensibly reliable people," said Dr. J. Allen Hynek. "To the best of my recollection even the 'antenna' shown on the back has been previously reported, as has the 'tail' structure," he added.

The bearded bespectacled Dr. Hynek, chairman of the astonomy department at Northwestern University near Chicago, has studied unidentified flying objects for more than a decade. He is scientific advisor to the Air Force's Project Blue Book, coordinator of all UFO reports for the military.

The press release then goes on to say that Dan Jaroslaw, who was seventeen at the time, and his brother Grant, who was fifteen, photographed the pictures with an inexpensive Polaroid camera. They snapped it between the ropes of a children's swing. The branches of a small bush appeared on one side and an iron pole on the other. The picture showed a "flying saucer" with a sort of tail fin and above this an antenna. The teenagers' home was near Selfridge Air Force Base, which reported it had no unusual radar sightings and its helicopters aloft at the time had spotted nothing.

The photographs were copied so they could be studied by the Project Blue Book staff and checked by Dr. Hynek's assistants. The important points here, aside from the fact that these pictures were taken, are: one, the Jaroslaw brothers were not subjected to ridicule; two, a noted scientist studied the prints and pronounced them genuine; three, the incident is being studied seriously by the Air Force.

So, people are changing their attitude about UFOs, and more are coming around to the idea that UFOs are a serious subject.

11

Contradictory Answers

SOME OF THE BEST sightings on record have drawn contradictory explanations from Air Force investigators and the people involved in the incidents. Both parties have stubbornly held to their opinions, and the reader can only make up his own mind who was right. The Exeter incident was one of these. Here are stories of four others.

On the morning of March 8, 1950, a Trans World Airlines plane circled the Dayton (Ohio) Municipal Airport in order to work into a landing pattern. Off to the southeast the pilot and co-pilot noticed a very bright light. The pilot radioed in a report.

The airport tower operator said, "We're watching it. We've alerted the Ohio National Guard. They're sending up a plane to get a closer look. Watch for it."

Even as he spoke, an Ohio National Guard pilot was heading for his F-51, his arms laden with a helmet, a parachute, and an oxygen mask.

118

The operator then notified the Air Technical Intelligence Center office at nearby Wright-Patterson Air Force Base of the bright light. The ATIC staff rushed outside and looked skyward. There it was, an extremely bright light, larger than a star.

The operator also notified the radar crew at the air base. The sergeant on duty replied that they had the "thing" located on the scope. They also had blips representing the airliner circling above and the F-51 as it lifted off the runway. Still another blip appeared on the screen as a second F-51 was dispatched from the air base. As soon as the second F-51 was airborne, the sergeant watching the radarscope contacted both F-51 pilots by radio. He vectored, or directed them toward their target.

The F-51s started climbing. By radio their pilots kept up a conversation with each other and with the radar technician. By this time one of the ATIC officers had rushed to the radar room and was watching the blips moving across the lighted radar screen. The sergeant had pointed out the unidentified blip so that the officer could keep track of it.

One pilot soon called in, "I see it!" Then the other did the same. Both climbed to 15,000 feet in pursuit. There they ran into thick clouds and lost sight of the UFO.

"You're closing in on it," the radar technician informed them.

The two pilots decided to spread out so they would not collide. They climbed higher.

"Watch out! You're almost on top of it!" the radar man warned.

"Icing fast. Visibility zero," both pilots reported. The chances of a midair collision were too high. Both sensibly nosed down until they emerged from the clouds. When they learned that the target was fading fast from the radarscope, they decided to land. On the way in, they heard that the UFO was gone from the radarscope and could no longer be seen from the ground.

The ATIC staff held a conference that afternoon. They did not include the pilots or the radar technician. After studying weather reports, they decided the bright light was merely the planet Venus. Ice clouds can produce some very strange effects on radarscopes, and the one the pilots ran into might have caused a distortion of the image of Venus, making it appear much closer than it actually was. Satisfied with this interpretation, ATIC sent word to the Pentagon. The UFO was officially identified as the planet Venus.

One of the F-51 pilots accepted this verdict. The other did not. He said, "What I saw was no planet. Before the clouds obscured it, I got a good look at it. It was round, it was huge, and it was metallic." However, his statement did not make the ATIC officers change their statement.

The radar technician also rejected the Venus explanation. However, he was only a sergeant and did not argue with his superior officers. He kept still for over two years. Then, when he was no longer in uniform, he visited ATIC headquarters and asked if he might see the report on this sighting. Captain Ruppelt was in charge of Project Blue Book by this time, and promptly supplied the folder of data.

After reading it, the former radar technician slammed it down. "Venus, my foot!" he exclaimed. Then he went on to say that he had worked a great deal with radar, even before World War II. He had helped with the operational tests on the first microwave warning radars developed by the Army. He added, "What I saw on the radarscope that day was no ice cloud. I've seen many return images from thunderclouds, ice clouds, and blips caused by temperature inversions. In such cases the return is always fuzzy, and varies in intensity of brightness. That day we had a good solid return on the scope. It was a return from a solid object. I say the return came from some type of aircraft."

Captain Ruppelt added these notes to the file. But to this day the verdict stands that the bright light seen over ATIC headquarters was the planet Venus.

Who was right, the Air Force or the radar technician and the pilot?

Another sighting for which the findings were contradictory occurred on November 5, 1957. At 5 A.M. the Coast Guard cutter *Sebago* was cruising in the Gulf of Mexico about two hundred miles south of the coast of Louisiana. At 5:10 A.M. the crewman scanning the radarscope on the bridge of the cutter reported locating an unidentified blip "at 246 degrees true, moving North to South, range 12,000 yards." or almost seven miles. The unidentified craft moved swiftly and then stopped and held its position. This ability to hover is something no conventional aircraft possessed at that time, though helicopters have it now. After hovering, the object speeded up, circled about, and stopped again at a position nearer the cutter.

The radar man notified the desk officer and the cutter's combat information center. The officer summoned three other officers and went out on deck.

"There it is!" one of them exclaimed. He trained powerful binoculars on the sky, but all he could see was a brilliant light. He tried hard to see whether there was the dark shadow of a structure behind the light but could not be sure. Neither could the others.

Meanwhile the radar man was keeping track and making notes. At 5:14 the unidentified blip streaked off the scope. At 5:16 it reappeared at a position 22 miles north of its former location. At 5:18 it faded off again, and at 5:20 reappeared and remained stationary at a position again seven miles north. At 5:21 the men on deck saw it visually for three to five seconds as a brilliant white object with no distinguishable shape. Then it disappeared into a cloudbank. At 5:37 the *Sebago* radarscope showed that the object was about 175 miles to the north. Then all contact was lost for good.

All this information was sent to Project Blue Book. The Air Force issued an explanation that some might have thought sounded repetitious. It said that the Coast Guardsmen had been watching a star or a meteor! The men from the cutter snorted because they believed no star or meteor could register the kind of movements revealed on the *Sebago's* radar screen.

Who was right? The Air Force or the cutter's crew?

Of course, half the fun of flying saucer and UFO sightings is that they can happen any time and any place, with never an advance warning. A person never knows when he is going to see one or the other. One teenager who agrees whole-heartedly with this is Harold Butcher of Cherry Creek, New York. Why, he wonders, with the whole of the earth to choose from, did a UFO slip down on his family's farm the evening of August 19, 1965? Here is the story of what Harold later said occurred.

Farm work varies from season to season, but cows have to be milked morning and night the year around. Since milking is a tedious chore, Harold had installed a radio in the main barn so he could listen to the lively music broadcast by radio station WKBW. This particular evening, which began no differently from hundreds of others, Harold went to the barn, turned on the radio, and started milking. There was a short newscast, and the announcer gave the time as 8:15 P.M., when Harold heard a commotion outside. He stood up and looked out an east window. In an adjoining field, as summer twilight was darkening, he saw the herd bull bellowing wildly and bending the pipe to which he was tethered. Small wonder! Overhead hovered a silver-colored, football-shaped object. Harold guessed it was about fifty feet long and maybe twenty feet thick. He could see two vertical side seams in the structure and a line of rivets along the seams. A reddish vapor was being discharged from the underside. As he watched breathlessly, the object moved horizontally. Yellowish vapor oozed from one of the ends, and the craft settled behind a large maple tree. At that moment, the radio program was completely washed out by static.

Harold raced outside and headed for the maple tree that grew atop a slight hill. When he was about opposite the bull, the UFO shot upwards and vanished. However, Harold had gotten close enough to hear a sort of beeping, or bizz-bizz noise from it.

He raced for the house, yelled about the UFO, and hurried outside again, followed by his fourteen-year-old brother, Robert. They saw the UFO just atop a pine grove on a neighboring farm. Once more it vanished, leaving a cloud of red vapor. By this time his mother, his older brother Bill, and a teenage neighbor girl had also come outside. They were too late to see anything.

Everyone talked excitedly, and Harold described what he had seen. Since her husband was away, Mrs. Butcher decided to call the police. The four of them went inside while she telephoned the Fredonia State Police Barracks. She was told a trooper would come immediately.

The group sat around talking, and then the neighbor girl said, "I'm going outside for another look." Almost immediately she raced back in, screaming, "It's here again!" In her excitement she ran into a younger child and knocked her down. The little girl began to cry, so Mrs. Butcher decided to stay and comfort her. The four teenagers ran outside. They saw the UFO hover over a field about 700 feet away. Then it moved in a south-easterly direction, giving off a glowing yellow vapor trail.

"Look at the green glow on the clouds above it," Harold pointed out.

The others saw this too. By looking very intently, they thought they could see the outline of the mysterious craft. A minute later it drifted out of sight. They kept watch, but it did not return.

Shortly after 9:15 P.M. two State Troopers arrived. The teenagers, with Harold in the lead, led them to the spot where he had first seen the UFO. "Boy, something smells funny around here," he exclaimed.

"It sure does," the others agreed. The odor was strong and sharp and rather unpleasant. No one could recall ever having smelled anything like it before.

With powerful flashlights the troopers went over the area. They found nothing unusual. "We'll check again tomorrow in the daytime," they promised, and left.

The next morning Harold did his chores. Then he returned to the site and saw a purple damp substance on the ground. He dipped his finger in it. It smelled like household lubricating oil. He hurried back to the barn for a shovel and a box, dug a shovelful of dirt and emptied it in the box. When the troopers arrived, he gave them the box.

While the police were still there, five officers of the Niagara Falls Air Force Base appeared. They questioned Harold over and over, and his family. When a reporter for the Buffalo *Evening News* interviewed them, they admitted they had no idea what the UFO could have been.

Days passed, and there was no word about the contents of the box. Mrs. Butcher called the troopers, who said they had given it to the military men. She called the air base and was told nothing. The family never did learn what the analysis proved, if anything. Although the Air Force made no official statement, the military investigators told the newspapers, "The four young people did see something." But what it was no one has yet explained.

An investigator for NICAP also questioned Harold and the others and was convinced the incident was not a hoax. It was reported in *The U.F.O. Investigator*.

Another puzzling incident was recorded the same night that the first Exeter sightings were made, this one in Texas. The time was 1 A.M.; the place, a field outside of Damon in Brazoria County, south of Houston. The observers were Chief Deputy B. E. McCoy and Patrol Deputy Robert Goode. Both worked out of the sheriff's office at nearby Angleton, Texas, and both were graduates of a police academy.

While on patrol on a bright moonlit night, the two said later, they saw a huge UFO come up to a pasture next to the highway. It was about 150 feet from their cruiser and, as Deputy Goode recalled later, "about telephone pole high." It appeared to be about 200 feet wide and 50 feet long, mostly gray in color, with a bright purple light on one wing tip and a small blinking blue light on the other. These lights illuminated the ground roundabout and even reflected into the patrol car. The object made no sound. The two lawmen took turns leaning out the windows, and viewing it with binoculars.

Suddenly the UFO nosed down and charged toward the car. The officers could see its shadow racing over the ground toward them. The shadow was almost as big as a football field. Officer Goode rammed the car into gear and sped away at a speed that mounted to 110 miles per hour. They got away from the UFO, or at least it did not follow them. But farther along the road they stopped, talked it over, and decided to return for another look. They simply could not believe what they had seen. Once more they saw the mysterious craft. When it shot straight up into the sky and disappeared, they returned to the sheriff's office and filed written reports of their experience.

The sheriff contacted nearby Ellington Air Force Base. An Air Force investigator named Major Laurence R. Leach, Jr., arrived to question the patrolmen. Afterward he wrote in the report which he sent on to Project Blue Book, ". . . There is no doubt in my mind that they definitely saw some unusual object or phenomenon. . . . Both officers appeared to be intelligent, mature, level-headed persons capable of sound judgment and reasoning."

The official Air Force explanation pointed out that the star Antares was setting at the time of the sighting and that there was a surface temperature inversion from ground level to 300 feet, and another from 8,000 to 10,500 feet. Since this latter inversion was strong enough to register on a radar set, it could have caused a distortion in the appearance of the star. But then the Air Force added, "The fact that the object disappeared by shooting up 90 degrees into the air makes this case unidentified since such an abrupt change in position prevents an astronomical explanation."

Deputy Goode doesn't agree that he could have

been looking at a star. He feels the only answer possible is that what he and his friend saw "was something from another planet."

A member of NICAP also gathered information which he sent on to the agency's headquarters. NICAP labels this sighting *Unexplained*.

Contradictions really mounted in mid-1965 after Police Officer Louis Sykes of Wynnewood, Oklahoma, first spotted a lighted object in the sky about 1:30 A.M. the morning of July 31. The UFO flashed red, blue and white lights. Sykes radioed in to the Oklahoma Highway Patrol, and then kept the UFO under observation for forty-five minutes. In the meantime the State Highway Patrol Officer at Oklahoma City was alerted, and he in turn notified Tinker Air Force Base nearby. The air base reported having the object located on its radarscope and also said there were no other aircraft aloft at that time so that the unidentified blip was the only one on the screen.

The next night, August 1, diamond-shaped formations of UFOs which changed colors from red to white were seen for forty minutes by patrolmen in three police cars cruising about Shawnee, Oklahoma. Oklahoma Highway Patrol Headquarters received so many calls from a wide area that its teletype was jammed. Its official report said the sightings came from Purcell north through the Norman area to Chandler and back through Meeker and Shawnee. It also stated, "Oklahoma Highway Patrol Units 30 and 40 have also made visual sightings. Tinker Air Force Base has had from one to four of them on radar at a time, and they advise they are flying very high at approximately 22,000 feet."

The UFOs were also sighted by numerous people in the area on the nights of August 2 and 3.

All this information was forwarded to Project Blue Book. A spokesman, not identified as Major Quintanella, issued a statement which said flatly, "There has been no confirmation that any of the sightings were tracked on radar." This person also ascribed the sightings to four stars in the constellation Orion.

Since the objects in question had been seen by numerous people, both law officers and civilians, there was considerable objection raised when the Air Force explanation was printed in the newspapers. It was an unfortunate statement because it contradicted the reports made by the Oklahoma State Highway Patrol and two air base radar reports. One newspaperman, who remains unidentified, contacted two of the nation's most prominent astronomers. He gave them all the evidence recorded about the sightings and told them of the Air Force identification of the UFOs. Then he asked these two scientists to study the evidence and give their opinions on the matter.

Here are their answers. Dr. Robert Risser of the Oklahoma Science and Art Planetarium is quoted as saying, "The Air Force assertion that these lights were nothing more than stars in the constellation Orion is about as far from the truth as you can get."

Professor Walter Webb, chief lecturer at the Hayden Planetarium in Boston, is quoted as saying, "At the time of these sightings the constellation Orion was visible only from the other side of the world."

Who do you think was right?

Equally contradictory answers cropped up
when space technicians and astronauts sighted
UFOs during various space launch programs.
Starting in 1961, rumors began circulating that
UFOs had appeared as unidentified blips on radarscopes tracking space launchings. Major Keyhoe, director of NICAP, tracked down the story
and described the happenings in an article published in January 1965 by *True* magazine. The
facts he revealed were never denied by the Air
Force.

According to Major Keyhoe, the story began
on January 10, 1961, in the radar room of the
National Aeronautics and Space Administration
(NASA) complex at Cape Canaveral, since renamed Cape Kennedy. A Polaris missile was to
be test-launched, and its progress tracked several
thousand miles out over the Atlantic Ocean. Television cameras carried pictures of the launching
center's operational room and launch platform
into millions of American homes. They photographed the dramatic skyward lift-off of the Polaris missile and followed it until it could no longer
be seen by the cameras.

What the cameras did not show was the startled
faces of the radar technicians as they monitored
their screens. Even before the missile completed
its initial climb, an unknown blip appeared on the
scope. It was bigger than the one for Polaris and
maneuvered close to it. In fact, it came so close
that the automatic tracking radar on the ground,
set to follow the missile, locked onto the UFO by
mistake. After keeping pace with the missile for
several moments, the UFO dropped back and

slipped out of radar range. It took the ground trackers fourteen minutes to lock onto Polaris again, and this time keep it under constant surveillance. The official tracking log of this launching confirms the appearance of the UFO. Neither NASA nor Air Force officials ever explained what it might have been.

Almost the same thing happened April 18, 1964, when the first two-man Gemini capsule was put into a planned orbit around the earth. This capsule carried instruments only, not astronauts. Its launching was a very important step in our long-range attempt to put a man on the moon. Once more millions of Americans watched the exciting blast-off on their television sets. They were given glimpses of rooms where computers, dials, clocks, microphones, and other technical machinery gathered data as the capsule soared around the earth.

However, as before, the cameras did not show the appearance of four UFO blips on the radar screens while the capsule was still in its first orbit. Four unidentified spacecraft closed in on the capsule and then took positions around it — one beneath, one behind, and two above it. They paced the capsule for a full orbit, then dropped back in orderly fashion and vanished out of radar range.

During the May 1963 orbit of Major Gordon Cooper through space, the astronaut radioed the tracking station at Muchea, Australia, that he had sighted a greenish object moving east to west. This is contrary to the orbits taken by man-made satellites. Nearly one hundred persons, some of them technicians, saw the UFO appear on the Australian radar. A commentator for the National

Broadcasting Company spread the word around the world. Naturally newsmen were very excited about this. But when they tried to question Cooper later, they were told that he could not issue any statement, and any word would have to come from NASA officials. Although newsmen pressed further for an explanation, none was ever forthcoming.

Then on June 4, 1965, James McDivitt and Edward White, our first two-man team of astronauts, went aloft. As they were moving eastward over the Hawaiian Islands, White was sleeping but McDivitt radioed that he had seen a weird object with armlike projections flash by and had taken a movie film of it with the camera mounted in the Gemini cabin. Later, after White had awakened, two more such objects were seen out over the Caribbean.

The Air Force issued an answer promptly. It said the objects were one and the same, our satellite Pegasus. But reporters who checked with the Spacetrack agency were told that Pegasus actually was 1,200 miles away from the Gemini capsule at the time of the sighting.

The mystery thickened when an official for NASA stated, "Careful study of the pictures taken by McDivitt of the object seen from the capsule shows nothing that looks like a satellite." When a still reproduction of one of the McDivitt movie frames was released for newspaper publication, it showed a disc-shaped object with a glowing trail behind it. But nothing more was said publicly about its identity.

Again in 1965, the team of Gemini Seven reported seeing a "bogey" on their second orbit. In airmen's vocabulary a bogey is an unidentified craft that could be hostile. The official at the NASA tracking station told Astronaut Frank Borman that he probably was looking at the burned out booster rocket that had lifted him and James Lovell into orbit.

Borman astonished all who were listening to the conversation on loud-speakers by saying that he could see the booster rocket *and* the bogey. Moments later the bogey dropped from sight.

When newsmen sought more information about the bogey, the Air Force stated that Borman was looking at the debris of a Titan rocket that had blown up weeks before. But a spokesman at the Spacetrack agency told reporters, "There is no rocket debris, Titan or otherwise, in that area at this time going in that direction at that altitude."

So one thing becomes very obvious. The contradictory answers described in this chapter point to the great need for a serious, scientific investigation of UFOs.

12

The Big Question

THE BIG QUESTION still remains: What is the real
nature of flying saucers and unidentified flying
objects?

The Air Force says that most are common astronomical objects and atmospheric phenomena
such as stars, meteors, balloons, mirages, marsh
gas, flocks of birds, earth satellites, reflections
off clouds, reflection of sunlight off shiny surfaces,
cloud formations, ball lightning, and radar reflections off temperature inversion layers in the atmosphere. It also maintains that most sightings
would be explained if the right kind of information were available about them.

Flying-saucer fans are equally positive that
UFOs are manned by visitors from outer space.
They poke fun at any who try to identify UFOs
as natural objects. This discourages many scientists and trained experts from tackling the UFO
mystery.

Scientists do point out that the chances of a
vehicle from outer space's penetrating the earth's
atmosphere and hovering or landing and taking

off again without detection are very, very small. Our sky is constantly scanned by radarscopes that show when an object passes through the earth's ionosphere. They can show whether the object is a natural one such as a meteor or an artificial one such as a satellite. Radar has been so refined that it is astonishingly sensitive. It can register the movement in the air of a single bee, or birds riding on high thermal currents, or the sea breeze as it moves across the land.

Scientists also say that the supersonic speeds at which UFOs are said to travel should cause sonic booms, yet most UFOs sighted move silently overhead. Their dizzy turns defy the force of the earth's gravity. No conventional aircraft could survive such turns; it would break into bits. This raises the question: Are UFOs constructed by supermen who have learned how to cancel the pull of gravity?

The North American Air Defense Command keeps track of more than 1,000 objects orbited by man into space. It has never reported one UFO. None have ever been seen or photographed through the giant telescope at the Mount Palomar Observatory in California or the Harvard Meteor Project. And yet, UFOs keep cropping up all over the world.

For fifteen years the Air Force has followed a debunk-and-ridicule policy toward UFO observers. Yet many sightings have been reported by scientifically trained or highly skilled people. Hundreds of "brain teasers" remain without adequate explanation. The Exeter incident, the B-29 sighting of the so-called "mother ship," and the UFOs trailing our space capsules are only a few of these.

Here is a more recent example, one hard to debunk or explain away as a star or fireball. On June 23, 1966, an Apollo Space Project flight engineer named Julian Sandoval claimed to have sighted a three-hundred-foot-long UFO near Albuquerque, New Mexico. Sandoval is a pilot and former Air Force navigator with 7,000 hours flying time to his credit. He has a very responsible position, being in charge of the electrical power and environmental control for Project Apollo.

Sandoval watched this UFO for 51 minutes, with and without binoculars. He said it was tetrahedral in shape and glowed like a light bulb. It had four blue-green lights at the tail. Whenever it changed position, the glow brightened. The sky was clear, the moon brilliant. Sandoval was able to estimate the UFO's size when it hovered over radio towers, which provided him with points of reference for measuring. For about 22 miles the UFO traveled at an average speed of 35 miles per hour. It slowly ascended, then deceded to about 9,000 feet. Finally it went into a vertical climb at a speed which Sandoval estimated at "Mach 6 [six times the speed of sound] or better."

Two other persons, one of them a police officer, confirmed this sighting.

Fortunately for Mr. Sandoval and other competent witnesses who are now, and will be, making public reports of their sightings of UFOs, the tide has changed against the debunk-and-ridicule policy. This has happened largely because of the campaign of members of NICAP and such individuals as Major Keyhoe and John Fuller to have flying saucers classified as serious business. NICAP does not provide the final answer. It has not solved any of the *Unexplainables*. It has produced no concrete evidence that UFOs are from outer space. Instead, it asks people to consider this possibility, and investigate the matter more thoroughly.

Recently Dr. J. Allen Hynek said, "Instead of having UFO a synonym for crackpot and ridicule, let's make it scientifically respectable. . . . We should put as much effort on one of these puzzling cases as we would on a Brinks robbery or a kidnap case." This statement comes from the renowned scientist who has been a chief UFO consultant for the Air Force for the past eighteen years.

Dr. Hynek also pointed out, "No true scientific investigation of the UFO phenomenon has ever been undertaken, despite the great volume of hard data." This deficiency is regrettable because as far back as July 20, 1962, when the Air Force issued official regulation #202-2, it stated, "There is need for further scientific knowledge in such fields as geophysics, astronomy, and physics of the upper atmosphere which the study and analysis of UFOs and similar aerial phenomena may provide." Yet the Air Force has done almost nothing to acquire this knowledge or, if it has, it has not made the results public.

NICAP has made a tremendous contribution in assembling information on sightings and letting the public know about them. It has weeded out the "crackpots" and has convinced many that flying saucers are worthy of serious study. In contrast, over the past ten years the Air Force has made only a small, halfhearted attempt to investigate sightings made through military channels.

Only late in 1966 did the Air Force begin to change its attitude.

In mid-October of that year it announced that $313,000 had been set aside for an independent scientific university study of UFO reports. The University of Colorado at Boulder was awarded the research project. In turn, it was to select several other universities to assist in the study. Dr. Edward U. Condon of the Department of Physics and Astrophysics was named director of the study. He has been assisted by specialists in the fields of psychology, engineering sciences, electrical engineering, astro-geophysics, sociology, atmospheric research, and behavorial science. These men will try to find clues as to whether UFOs are figments of the imagination, intelligently guided vehicles from planets other than Earth, or natural phenomena not yet fully understood. They will undertake a systematic study of the physical, psychological, and social phenomena associated with responsibly reported UFO sightings. None of these men has any preconceived notions that UFOs are nonsense or that they contain visitors from outer space. They hope to be as strictly objective as possible in examining the records of the Air Force and of NICAP.

The National Academy of Sciences will name a panel to review the Colorado report when completed in 1968.

No doubt this study will produce some interesting information. It certainly is a big step in the right direction and a serious attempt to gain more information about UFOs. Perhaps it will help us understand them better. Still, the author feels that we will never have proof as to the real existence of the structured UFOs until one lands or crashes so the craft, its equipment and occupants, if any, can be examined thoroughly.

The Air Force position on UFOs now is this. "The Air Force does not deny the possibility that some form of life may exist on other planets in the universe. However, to date, the Air Force has neither received nor discovered any evidence which proves the existence or intraspace mobility of extraterrestrial life." In other words, the Air Force still says there is no proof that we on earth are receiving visits from creatures or aircraft from outer space.

Up to this moment no concrete proof has ever turned up as to the real identity of UFOs. We don't have a single clue as to what they are, or who they are, or where they come from, or why they are here. We only feel sure that they are not secret weapons belonging to us or any other country.

None of the UFOs seen has ever seemed to pose a threat to our country. But until we learn exactly what the *Unexplainables* are, the Air Force will be ever on guard. NICAP will continue assembling information from reliable observers. Scientists will study the problem. More and more people will be given special training on aerial phenomena so they will be more skillful observers.

Someday we are bound to discover the truth.

But until that day comes, we will be entertained and excited and puzzled by one of the great mysteries of the twentieth century.

Index